Working with Young Runaways
Learning from practice

Gwyther Rees

The Children's Society

First published in 2001

The Children's Society
Edward Rudolf House
Margery Street
London WC1X 0JL

A catalogue record of this book is available from the British Library.

ISBN 1 899783 39 3

Contents

ACKNOWLEDGEMENTS

This report has been published by The Children's Society with the kind co-operation of the NSPCC, Barnardo's, the Catholic Children's Society and ASTRA.

Many thanks are due to the practitioners and managers who contributed their views to this publication:

ASTRA: Keith Harrison*; Barnardo's: Ginny Wilkinson, Mel Thornton, Rachel Holden; Catholic Children's Society: Ruth Kirkpatrick; NSPCC: Lucy Titheridge, Nora Duckett; The Children's Society: Alison Jeremy, Andrew Gilyead, Andrew Lloyd, Andrew Taylor, Andy McCullough, Chris Manson, Dave Roberts, Guy Thompstone, Jane Osburn, Janice Horton, Jenny Lee*, Jill Corbin, Jill Greenfield, Katy Evdokiou, Mark Lee, Mary Flynn, Martine Osmond, Mike Huett, Penny Dean, Rebecca Holmes, Sheila Wood, Tracey Thompson, Ulfat Riaz, Vivien Lewis.

(Contributors marked with an asterisk were no longer employed by their respective organisations at the time when they were interviewed.)

I am also very grateful to the panel of internal and external readers who provided valuable feedback on various drafts of the report: Patricia Durr, Mark Lee, Penny Dean, Jean Trewhitt (The Children's Society), Professor Mike Stein (University of York), Nick Frost (University of Leeds), Kath Tunstall (Leeds Social Services), Bryan Evans (Aberlour Childcare Trust).

1

INTRODUCTION

The phenomenon of children and young people running away from home or care has, over the past two decades, gradually become recognised as an important social policy issue in the UK. This recognition has been due to the development of projects working with this target group and the publication of research findings into their needs.

This report is the first to present an overview of the models of practice that have been developed in the UK in recent years to work specifically with these young people. Its primary intention is to draw together the learning from these practice models in order to inform the future development of work with this target group.

Background, aims and methods

Background

The report was commissioned by The Children's Society to fill a gap in publications about the issue of children and young people running away. There have been a number of research-based publications on this topic in the UK over the past 20 years, but no substantial detailed account of the way in which projects have been working with this target group.

All known projects working specifically with these young people, outside The Children's Society, were invited to contribute their views and experiences to the report and, ultimately, five external projects and six internal projects participated in this piece of work. The report incorporates learning from most of the projects that have been in existence in the UK from the early 1980s onwards. The comprehensive nature of the report's coverage has been possible thanks to the co-operation of a number of organisations outside The Children's Society – namely, Barnardo's, the NSPCC, the Catholic Children's Society and the ASTRA Project (Alternative Solutions to Running Away).

This first UK practice-based publication on the issues involved in working with children and young people is published at a time when the Social Exclusion Unit is conducting a consultation exercise on young runaways and the Department of Health is preparing guidance on working with young people who go missing. It is hoped that the information provided here will complement these other initiatives and provide some indications of ways forward in developing a better response to the needs of children and young people who run away from their families or from substitute care.

It is important that this publication is also seen within the context of an ongoing programme of dissemination of practice learning, research and evaluation related to the issue of children and young people running away that is being undertaken by The Children's Society and partner organisations in Scotland and Northern Ireland, utilising Children's Promise funding. The programme's first product was the publication of the first comprehensive UK report on this issue in 1999 (Safe on the Streets Research Team, 1999), some of the key findings of which are summarised in Chapter 2. That report presented the results of research involving young people and professionals from the statutory and voluntary sectors working with them in 27 areas of the UK. Individual country reports for Scotland, Northern Ireland and Wales, emanating from the research, are currently being prepared. Another key element of the programme is the first large-scale evaluation to be undertaken in the UK of projects working with this target group. This research project currently involves nine projects operating a range of practice models, and will gather perspectives from young people, project staff, professionals in other agencies, and parents and carers. Results from the evaluation will be disseminated in late 2003.

Aims

The current publication focuses on the views and experiences of managers and practitioners who have worked in projects targeted specifically at young runaways. The intention is not to pre-empt the above multi-perspective evaluation, but to summarise the considerable expertise that has been developed within these projects and to make this expertise accessible to a wide audience.

The main intended audience for the report is managers and policy-makers in the statutory and voluntary sectors who may be considering developing services to meet the needs of young people who run away. The aim is to provide an overview of the issues involved in initiating, developing and managing projects and services that work with this target group.

Although the report does not provide a detailed account of day-to-day practice, it is hoped that the second half (Chapters 8 to 12) will also be of value to practitioners who, as part of their day-to-day work, are engaged with young people who run away.

Methods

The primary source of information for the report has been the expertise and views gathered from managers and practitioners who work or have worked in projects aimed at children and young people who run away. A total of 32 practitioners and managers within the 11 projects contributed their views by means of audio-recorded semi-structured interviews. The contributors had worked extensively with this target group as well as having had a wide range of previous experience of work with children and young people in the statutory and voluntary sectors.

This method of information gathering yielded a wealth of material for the publication. However, it is important to acknowledge that the views expressed in this report are almost entirely from the voluntary sector. The relevance of these views stems from the fact that the large majority of practice development aimed specifically at young runaways has taken place within this sector. Clearly, there is also the need to gather views on the work of the projects from statutory sector professionals and this will happen as part of the evaluation programme described earlier.

The interviews were analysed and an initial draft report was prepared. Relevant parts of the draft were circulated to all contributors for comment and to ensure that their views had been accurately and fully represented. A panel of readers, consisting of internal staff, external representatives from statutory and voluntary sector organisations, and academics, were also invited to comment on the complete draft. Comments from contributors and readers were incorporated into the final draft. All direct quotes have been approved by contributors prior to finalisation of the report.

Structure of the report

This introductory chapter offers a brief recent historical overview of the development of work with children and young people who run away, and a summary of the current situation in terms of services and legislation.

Chapter 2 provides a summary of the key research findings from the UK and elsewhere in relation to the target group

Chapters 3 to 7 look at the range of practice models that have been developed in the UK to date, including refuges, street work, missing persons schemes, centre-based models and preventive work.

Chapters 8 to 12 explore a number of issues general to all work with the target group: approaches to working with children and young people, inter-agency working, anti-discriminatory practice, staffing and management, and developmental issues.

Chapter 13 summarises the key points of the report and makes suggestions and recommendations for future development.

The Appendix provides examples of alternative practice models that have been developed in other countries to work with children and young people who run away or are on the streets.

Note on terminology

In this report, the term 'running away' is used to describe children and young people who spend time away from home without the consent of parents or carers, or because they have been forced to leave by parents or carers. It normally refers to young people who have spent at least one night away from home. The term therefore encapsulates a number of other terms such as 'going missing', 'being thrown out', 'absconding', and so on.

The term 'young people' refers, unless clearly specified otherwise, to children and young people under the age of 18. There are substantial legal differences between young people under 16 and those aged 16 to 17 in terms of running away. However, most of the discussion in this report applies equally to young people in both these age groups.

The term 'contributor' refers to those people who contributed their views to this report (listed on the title page of the report), mainly by means of face-to-face or telephone interviews.

The term 'contributing project' refers to the 11 projects which agreed to contribute to the report (listed on the title page of the report).

A brief history

The recent history of work with young people who run away in the UK can probably be viewed as beginning with the development of the first refuge for young runaways in London in the early 1980s. This development stemmed from the recognition among agencies working with homeless people in the centre of London that there was a growing number of young people under the age of 16 on the streets. These young people could not legally be accommodated by hostels and night shelters (see the section on the legal framework, below, for an explanation of this).

The first UK refuge

The Children's Society convened a number of meetings with representatives from key statutory and voluntary agencies including Centrepoint, Westminster Social Services Department, the police, etc.) and also conducted a visit to a young person's refuge in the Netherlands. After four years of discussion and planning, the Society opened the country's first refuge for runaways – the Central London Teenage Project – in 1985. Initially, and for most of its life span, the refuge was technically acting outside the law in providing short-term accommodation for under-16s, but had the backing of the Metropolitan Police and Westminster Social Services, as well as non-statutory agencies. More details of the early history of this project are to be found in Newman (1989).

Part of the initial brief of the project was also to undertake research to learn more about the issue of young people running away. Monitoring information was gathered from young people using the refuge and in-depth interviews were carried out with some of them. A survey of police authorities was also conducted in order to collate information on reports of missing young people. The results of this research were published in Newman (1989). It was estimated that every year there were 98,000 reported incidents of young people under the age of 18 running away in the UK. This research, and the experience of working with young people at the London refuge, indicated that running away was a widespread phenomenon and that many of the young people on the streets in London had come from outside the capital.

Early practice developments outside London

In view of this information, The Children's Society launched its 'Young People Under Pressure' initiative which aimed to set up projects in a variety of locations throughout England and Wales to work with young people who ran away. This initiative eventually produced five additional projects in Birmingham, Manchester, Leeds, Bournemouth and Newport (Gwent). The Birmingham project, Youth Link, was the first to open, in 1988. Its initial service consisted of detached work[1] (see Chapter 4 for further details) and drop-in centre work with young people on the streets in Birmingham city centre. Safe in the City began work with young people in Manchester a year later, also focusing on detached city centre street work.

The other three projects in the initiative provided accommodation for young people along with other services. In 1989 Southside in Bournemouth began providing refuge for young people aged under 18, and also ran a drop-in centre. Leeds Safe House, which opened in 1991, provided a residential refuge along similar lines to the Central London Teenage Project. In 1993 the Porth Project started working with young people in South Wales, providing accommodation through a network of refuge foster carers linked by a central daytime centre-based staff team.

When the Southside refuge and Leeds Safe House opened they also were acting

---

1 Detached work is ongoing work with young people wherever they are

outside the legislative framework at that time. However, in the preceding years The Children's Society had spearheaded a campaign to obtain legal recognition for the role of refuges in providing short-term accommodation for young people under 16 who were away from home. This campaign led to the incorporation of provisions in the Children Act 1989. Section 51 of that Act allowed for legitimised refuges to be exempt for short periods from the laws on harbouring young people away from home. This meant that refuges for runaways could, without parental permission, provide accommodation for young people under the age of 16 who had run away from home for a continuous period of up to 14 nights. The Children Act 1989 became law in October 1991, and in the subsequent two years, the four Children's Society projects which provided refuge in London, Leeds, Bournemouth and Newport became certificated under Section 51 of the Act.

Thus by the mid-1990s there was a network of projects providing a variety of accommodation and other services for young people under 16 who had run away from family or substitute care. The early work of four of these services is described in Stein, Rees and Frost (1994).

Research studies in the early 1990s

The early 1990s also saw an increase in research activity in this field. A second survey of police statistics of missing persons was carried out by NCH – Action for Children (Abrahams and Mungall, 1992). The results of this survey broadly confirmed Newman's earlier projections, with estimates of 102,000 incidents a year of missing persons under 18 years of age in England and Scotland. In the following year, the results of the first survey to gather information directly from young people were published by The Children's Society (Rees, 1993). This survey estimated that in Leeds around one in seven young people ran away from home (or were forced to leave) and stayed away for at least one night, before the age of 16. A year later the Society published the findings of research into the work of Youth Link, Safe in the City, Leeds Safe House and the Porth Project (Stein, Rees and Frost, 1994). This study drew attention to the extreme levels of detachment experienced by some young people who ran away. Among a sample of 31 young people using the four projects, the researchers had interviewed seven young people who had spent continuous periods of six months or more away from family or substitute care before the age of 16.

Practice and research developments in the second half of the 1990s

The second half of the 1990s saw the development of new services by other non-statutory agencies and two further research studies. In 1995 Centrepoint, in partnership with the NSPCC, opened a new refuge in London, following the closure of the original London refuge the previous year. This was followed by a research report on young people using the refuge (Barter, 1996).

The issue of young people running away from residential care has had a high profile since the early surveys by Newman (and Abrahams and Mungall) had shown a particularly high prevalence among this small group of young people. In response to this, the Department of Health commissioned a major research study into the issue (Wade et al, 1998).

Also in 1998, the ASTRA project was established in Gloucester by a multi-agency consortium. The project offers support to young people who have been reported missing to the police and have returned home. Schemes working along similar lines have more recently been developed by Barnardo's in Yorkshire and the Midlands, working with young women who may be at risk of becoming involved in prostitution, and, in several locations, by The Children's Society.

In 1999 The Children's Society published the results of the largest piece of research yet carried out into the issue of young people running away in the UK (Safe on the Streets Research Team, 1999). It consisted of a survey of over 13,000 young people in 25 areas of the UK, and in-depth interviews with over 200 young people who had experience of running away. The results of this and the other research mentioned above are summarised in Chapter 2.

The current situation in the UK

This section provides a brief overview of current service provision for young people who run away in the UK, and a summary of the relevant law.

Current service provision

The current situation is rather fluid, with a number of recent and planned developments. There are now a range of models of working with young people who run away, or are at risk of running away, from primary prevention through to detached street work. The following is a list of known projects working exclusively or primarily with this target group in the UK. (There are, of course, many other projects which provide services for, and may work with, significant numbers of young people who run away as part of a wider target group. These include children's rights services, advocacy services, drop-in centres, family mediation services, and so on.)

In Manchester, Safe in the City (The Children's Society) provides a range of services including street work, an accessible project-base with a range of facilities, specialist teams working with black young people and young people who are being sexually exploited, a missing persons scheme, and preventive group work with young people in residential care.

The Bradford Young Missing Persons Scheme (Barnardo's), which was originally an offshoot of the Streets and Lanes Project (aimed at young women being sexually exploited) runs a missing persons scheme for young women and is developing an independent interview service for young people in residential care.

Safe on the Streets – Leeds (The Children's Society) runs a missing persons scheme and a preventive peer counselling scheme in schools, and is planning to develop a family group conferencing model. It is also carrying out research into the needs of black young people and lesbian, gay and bisexual young people who run away, which will feed into ongoing development of the project.

The Kirklees SOS Scheme (Barnardo's) does missing persons work with young women, with a focus on the prevention of sexual exploitation.

In Birmingham, Youth Link (The Children's Society) provides street work, a drop-in centre, a missing persons scheme, and a website and e-mail Internet service for young people focused on the issue of running away.

In Gloucester, the ASTRA Project (run by a consortium of local agencies) provides a missing persons scheme aimed at reducing repeat incidence of running away.

In London, there are several projects. The London Refuge (St Christopher's

Fellowship/NSPCC) is currently the only refuge in the UK operating under Section 51 of the Children Act. The London Streetwork Project (The Children's Society) is developing missing persons schemes and centre-based work, and is contributing to the development of a city-wide network. The Breaking Free Project (NSPCC) does work with young women on the streets who are being sexually exploited or who are at risk of being in this situation. The Home & Away Project (Catholic Children's Society) has a drop-in advice centre and does family-based work with young people who have run away or are at risk of running away, as part of a project working with 13- to 20-year-olds, and also provides a limited amount of short-term emergency accommodation.

In Weymouth, WAVES (The Children's Society) has a specialist under-16s worker as part of a project working with young people.

In Torquay, Checkpoint (The Children's Society) includes the South Coast Runaways Initiative which does centre- and community-based work, is developing an independent interview scheme for young people running away from residential care, and aims to provide emergency accommodation in the near future.

In Wales, Two Way Street (The Children's Society) in Cardiff runs a drop-in centre, does street work and is piloting a missing persons scheme.

In Scotland, the Aberlour Childcare Trust is currently developing the 'Running – Other Choices' project in Glasgow, which will offer a range of services aimed at working with young people who have run away or are at risk of running away.

The legal framework

The legal status of young people away from home or care under the age of 18 can be rather confusing and is, in certain cases, open to interpretation. Basically, the law applies differently to different groups of young people and there are also some variations between countries within the UK.

Looking first at the situation in England and Wales, there are three different groups. The first consists of young people under the age of 18 who are either on a care order, an emergency protection order or in police protection. For this group, Section 49 of the Children Act 1989 states that is an offence to assist them in running away or to keep them away from a responsible person who has legal care of them.

For other young people there is a difference in legal position according to age. Young people under 16 cannot leave home (even with parental consent) unless another adult takes responsibility for them, although it is not clear what sanctions there might be in relation to anyone accommodating a young person in this group while away from home. Section 2 of the Child Abduction Act 1984 states that anyone who 'takes or detains' a young person under the age of 16 who has run away may be prosecuted, but this may be deemed not to apply where a young person has chosen to run away and stay away with someone.

Young people aged 16 and 17, on the other hand, can leave home and live independently with parental consent, and Section 2 of the Child Abduction Act 1984 does not apply.

In practice, the application of the law is clearer. Essentially, anyone in one of the first two above groups who has run away will be returned home if found by the police, but in normal circumstances young people in the third group will not.

The legal situation in Northern Ireland is broadly the same as described above for

England and Wales. In relation to harbouring or abduction, the relevant piece of legislation is the Children (Northern Ireland) Order 1995.

In Scotland, the situation is different, particularly because it has a different definition of a 'child'. Legally, a child is someone who is under 16 or is subject to statutory supervision in terms of Section 70 of the Children (Scotland) Act 1995. Anyone not in the above two categories, and therefore the large majority of young people aged 16 and 17 who are not under statutory supervision, can legally leave home without parental permission. For under-16s, the situation remains similar to that for England and Wales, with the relevant legislation on harbouring being contained in Section 71 of the Social Work (Scotland) Act 1968.

In addition to the technicalities of legal status, there are other practical differences between young people under and over 16 years. There is a limited amount of hostel and emergency accommodation for young homeless people, which is only accessible to young people aged 16 and above, and there may be circumstances in which a young homeless person of 16 or 17 can also gain access to benefits. Neither of these possibilities is open to young people under the age of 16 who run away.

The only emergency accommodation that is legally available to young people under the age of 16 without parental consent is a certificated refuge, as discussed in the historical overview earlier in this chapter. The relevant legislation is contained within Section 51 of the Children Act 1989 (in relation to England and Wales), Section 38 of the Children (Scotland) Act 1995 and Article 70 of the Children (Northern Ireland) Order 1995. There is only one such refuge currently in operation in the UK.

The options open to young people who run away under the age of 16 are therefore extremely limited. They have no legitimate means of earning money in order to survive and there is currently only one accommodation project in the whole country that can legally provide them with accommodation without parental consent.

2

SUMMARY OF RECENT RESEARCH

This chapter provides a brief overview of the key research findings from published studies regarding young people running away. It draws primarily on recent UK studies, but makes some reference to findings from other countries, as indicated, on areas where current UK knowledge is lacking. All findings not specifically referenced are from Safe on the Streets Research Team (1999).

There are two reasons for providing this overview. First, findings from the research are referred to in various parts in the report. Second, some of the findings have clear implications for working practices with young people, and therefore can in themselves be of use to those seeking to develop services in this field.

Numbers of young people running away

It is estimated that one in nine young people will run away, or be forced to leave home, and stay away for at least one night, before the age of 16. This translates into about 77,000 young people running away for the first time each year in the UK, and about 129,000 incidents of running away.

There is no evidence of significant geographical variation between the countries which make up the UK, or between areas differentiated on the basis of population density or economic prosperity.

Characteristics of young people who run away

Not surprisingly, the likelihood of running away increases with age and most incidents happen between the ages of 13 and 15. However, around one in four young runaways had first run away before the age of 11, and these young people are more likely than average subsequently to run away away repeatedly.

Females are more likely to run away than males but the differences, although significant, are not of any great practical relevance. In any case, males who run away are likely to do so more often than females, so in terms of incidence there is a fairly even gender split.

There are, however, significant differences in running away rates for young people of different ethnic origins. Young white people are more likely to run away than young people from minority ethnic backgrounds. The estimated rates of running away are shown in Figure 1 (see page 10).

Some further findings in relation to young people from minority ethnic backgrounds are presented in Chapter 10.

Young people living in substitute care are far more likely than other young people

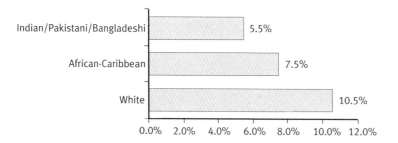

Figure 1: Estimated rates of running away for young people in the main ethnic groups

to run away. An estimated 45 per cent of these young people have run away at some point in their lives, and there is a high rate of repetitive incidence among this group. However, around half these young people will have started running away before entering the care system.

Reasons for running away

About four in five young people who ran away categorised themselves as having run away, and one in five as having been forced to leave home. For those young people who run away, the primary immediate reasons for running away are located in the home environment, as shown in Figure 2 (see below).

There is substantial evidence that in the case of many young people who run away there are long-term problems both within and outside the home which form the background to their running away. Looking at factors within the home, young people living in step-families and lone-parent families are significantly more likely to run away than young people living with both birth parents. Independent of this link

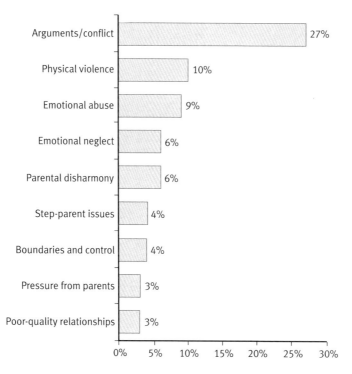

Figure 2: Main immediate triggers for running away given by young people

is the fact that young people with poor-quality relationships are significantly more likely to run away (irrespective of which family form they live in).

In general, factors outside the home play a much less substantial role in causing young people to run away. However, some young people cite personal or school problems as leading to or contributing to their running away.

There is only weak evidence of a link between family economic status and running away and this appears to be a relatively minor factor, compared with family form and the quality of family relationships.

For young people in substitute care there are two broad groups with different reasons for running away (Wade et al, 1998). One group are primarily running away because of 'pull' factors outside the care placement – usually running away in order to spend time with friends or family. The other group run away because of factors within the placement or to do with personal difficulties.

Links with other issues

There is strong evidence of significant links between running away and many other problems and issues in young people's lives. Young people who run away have significantly higher rates than other young people of self-reported depression, alcohol and drug problems, offending, and problems with peers. They also have significantly higher rates of problems at school, including truancy, exclusion, being bullied and difficulties with learning (see Figure 3, below).

Notably, despite the evidence that young people who run away have long-term problems at home, and potentially a range of difficulties in other areas of their lives, there is limited evidence of agency involvement before running away starts, with the obvious exception of young people who were living in substitute care.

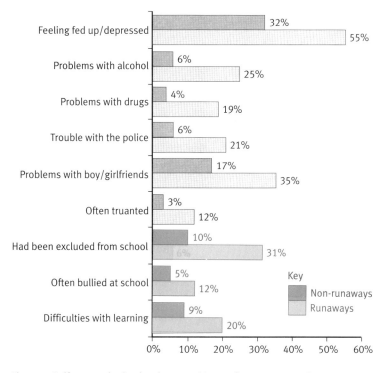

Figure 3: Self-reported school and personal issues for runaways and non-runaways

Experiences while away

It is clear from young people's accounts that being away from home can be a liberating and positive experience. Many young people felt that it had given them time to think, provided a respite, and helped them to sort out their problems. (See Figure 4, below.)

On the other hand, running away can be a risky and frightening experience for young people. Around a quarter of young people slept rough while they were away and around one in seven reported being sexually or physically assaulted while away.

Most young people stayed in their locality, slept at friends' or relatives' homes and were only away from home for a few nights. At the other end of the scale, research has provided evidence of young people being completely detached from home or care for six months or more, and relying on begging, stealing, dealing in drugs, having sex for money, or support from adult acquaintances in order to survive.

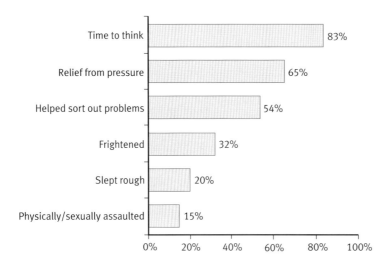

Figure 4: Experiences while away from home

Sub-groups of young people who run away

Most of the above findings relate to all young people who run away overnight. Inevitably there is considerable diversity within this group of young people. Safe on the Streets Research Team (1999) identified four broad sub-groups within the overall population of young people who run away or are forced to leave home under the age of 16.

1. Young people who run away once or twice, but who have not spent a night away from home. From the survey we would estimate that around 6 per cent of the total population of young people have this experience before the age of 16. This amounts to some 45,000 young people per school year.

2. Young people who run away once or twice, including spending one or more nights away from home. There are an estimated 9 per cent of young people in this category, amounting to 65,000 young people per school year.

3. Young people who run away repeatedly (three times or more), but do not become detached. About 2 per cent of all young people have this experience before the age of 16, numbering around 15,000 young people per school year.

4. Young people who become detached from home and substitute care for six months or more. It is not possible to estimate the size of this group of young people, but two UK qualitative studies have identified a number of young people who fit into this category (Stein, Rees and Frost, 1994; Safe on the Streets Research Team, 1999).

The reasons for running away and experiences of being away vary considerably between these four groups. The following four case studies, drawn from Safe on the Streets Research Team (1999), provide some illustration of these diverse experiences. The first two (Carlton and Anne) relate to young people who have only run away once or twice from family and substitute care; the third (Sian) is illustrative of a young person who has run away repeatedly and the final case study (Debbie) relates to young people who experience detachment.

CASE STUDY 1

Carlton

Carlton lived with his mother, father and younger brother up to the age of ten. He had suffered repeated sporadic abuse from his father since a young age, and matters came to a head:

> 'One day when I came in from school he just started shouting at me for no reason at all. Then he started to beat the hell out of me... My mum said that he didn't do it, that I did it myself. How could I do it myself on my back? I had to walk out... I ran away and stayed at a friend's house.'

Carlton stayed away for one night. Then he spoke to his mother and she said that she had asked the father to leave home, so Carlton returned. However, within a year the father moved back in:

> 'My dad came back. My mum had him back and he was cruel to me. He started drinking and his violence was unbearable. He was violent towards all of us.'

Eventually, at the age of 14, Carlton could not cope any more and he ran away for the second time:

> 'I couldn't bear his violence, couldn't forgive mum for letting him stay with us. I slept on a park bench with my jacket – no blanket or nothing. I stole food from shops. Sometimes I went home for food when dad was out.'

Carlton was picked up by the police after about a week away and placed in care, where he remained until he was 16.

CASE STUDY 2

Anne

Anne entered care with her siblings at an early age due to her mother's inability to cope. After several moves she went to live in a foster home with her brother. She was very close to him and felt a sense of responsibility towards him. Both Anne and her brother were physically abused by their foster parent over a period of time. Fear of further punishment prevented her from running away:

'I couldn't run away from foster care [as my foster carer] would have whacked me. I sat back once and watched her break my brother's nose. Probably if I'd run away from there she would have broke my legs so I couldn't run any more.'

Despite telling her social worker what was happening, nothing was done until her foster parent decided she would have to leave. When the placement broke down she was separated from her brother and given a placement in a children's home. Anger and anxiety at her past abuse, her separation from her brother and the failure of social services to act combined with dislike of her new surroundings. At 14 she ran away for the first and only time:

'The only time they did something was when I ran away from the [children's home]. I just thought to myself, "Where's my life going?" I didn't even like it there, so I ran away. Everyone used to run away from there. Nobody likes moving out of places and going to new places, not at the age of 14, when you've moved enough. Guinness Book of Records, me, for moving so much!'

She stayed out all night with others from the unit until she was picked up by the police and returned the next day. She felt the reaction of staff when she returned was initially unsympathetic; that, because running away was commonplace, they failed to explore the unhappiness that underpinned her absence:

'You run away and when you go back they don't sympathise with you, they just say to you, "Oh no, you shouldn't." I got grounded for it as well [for running away], just because I was unhappy. It were bad, so I didn't do it again. Because they moved me to another children's home. I loved it there.'

However, running away did eventually generate some action. She made a planned move to another children's home where she was to settle. She liked the fact that it felt less institutionalised, each child had their own room, and the staff were friendly and supportive. However, looking back she still felt some anger that she had to run away in order to draw attention to her unhappiness:

'You shouldn't have to run away from somewhere just to make a young child happy.'

CASE STUDY 3

Sian

Sian lived with her mother, her father and her younger brother. She has an older brother and sister who already lived away from home. She feels she never got on with her parents and that her brother was always favoured over herself, as her father had been in the army and expected that his son would follow in his footsteps. Sian described her father as 'a control freak'. There was a lack of communication between herself and her mother, to the point where 'it was difficult to sit in the same room'. At 12/13 Sian got into company of which her father didn't approve because they were going out with boys, drinking and taking drugs. There were big arguments.

The first time she left, it was because she had been out drinking with friends when she was 13. Her father grounded her:

'I stormed out the house and didn't go back. I went down the industrial estate and slept in a lorry, a big truck it was, at about 11 at night. I felt frightened. There were noises and it was cold. I went home three in the afternoon. I'd had nothing to eat. They [her parents] just ignored me. After a while we started talking again and started arguing. They just blamed me for everything.'

Sian said she had lost count of how many times she had stayed away overnight and that it was 20 or more times between the ages of 13 and 15. Sometimes she and friends would stay with older lads who had the tenancy of a flat on one of the estates. They would drink cider and use whatever drugs were available. Sometimes she would just walk around all night. She hated school and truanted 'nearly every day' from the age of 14.

When she was 15 she and a friend stayed away for a week. They stayed with friends and camped out as it was in the summer. She went home after a week and there was a terrible argument and on this occasion her father became violent and threw her out. After that Sian moved in with her aunt:

'I went to live with my auntie. She gave me more freedom than my parents did. It was easier for me.'

Sian said that staying with her auntie, she didn't need to go missing any more. About her parents she said:

'They blame me for everything, and they think that all the things I have done have affected their lives and they think that only they've got problems. When I see them out now they just walk past me and don't speak.'

Debbie

Debbie was living with her mother, stepfather, brother and two stepsisters. Her stepfather treated Debbie and her brother differently from the stepsisters, who were his biological children. He was violent towards Debbie and her brother. She says she used to get into trouble just to get her mother's attention:

'I didn't get on with my stepdad. It was because he fetched us up differently from the others. He used to give us real hidings, too. I used to be scared to go in the house. And people used to say, "And he's not your real dad anyway" and that would do my head in because my mum would never tell us who our real dad was.

'I didn't get on with my stepfather. I ran away at 14 to stay with friends and wouldn't go to school. My mum didn't even bother to look for me. I don't have any contact with her now.

'At first I slept at friends' houses and once I had to sleep in a shed for three nights.'

Debbie survived through shoplifting, a 'skill' she had learned before she left home when she had felt that she wasn't getting the things she needed. After a period of staying with friends and sleeping rough, she moved in with a heroin dealer whom she didn't even like. She just had nowhere else to go:

'I went and stayed with this lad who was a smack dealer. I didn't know anything about heroin until then. I didn't want to stay with him but I had nowhere else to go and the police were after us. I didn't even like him. Then I started taking it because he was taking it. I've been on it for four years now.

'I was away all the time from when I was 14. I've lived in seven houses with this lad but we were never settled because he was a dealer.'

Debbie phased out her school attendance after she ran away from home at the age of 14:

'I used to go to the teachers and they would give me jobs to do like taking notes. I couldn't do any work. I couldn't concentrate, that's why. So I stopped going to school at all. I don't think I was even on the register after a while.'

Long-term consequences of running away

Research into the long-term consequences of running away is relatively sparse in the UK. There is some evidence of a link between running away under the age of 16 and subsequent homelessness after the age of 16, and of a link with long-term social exclusion for those who run away repeatedly from a young age. It also seems that there is a strong link between running away and subsequently becoming involved in prostitution.

Findings from North America paint a bleak picture of the potential long-term outcomes for young people who run away. Young people who have experience of running away or being on the streets under the age of 18 are more likely to have an early pregnancy;[2] to become involved in survival sex;[3] to become HIV-positive;[4] to attempt suicide;[5] to have mental health problems;[6] and to develop problems with drugs, alcohol and other substances.[7]

It cannot be assumed that all these findings will translate to the UK context, but it is notable that most of the findings on running away in the UK summarised earlier in this chapter are very similar to those for the USA and Canada. The samples on which the above North American studies are based were often accessed through projects for runaways and the findings are therefore likely to be most applicable to young people who run away repeatedly and spend extended periods away from home.

Concluding comments

Research indicates that the incidence of running away is widespread in the UK and cuts across geographical, national and ethnic groupings. While for many young people running away may be a relatively minor incident in their lives, there is evidence that it is often an indicator of serious problems in the home environment, often of a long-term nature, together with a potential range of other difficulties and issues in the young person's life. The research emphasises the need to intervene early in young people's lives in order to prevent running away or to reduce repeat incidences.

The risks of running away in the short term are not inconsiderable, particularly for those young people who spend extended periods away from home. There is also some tentative evidence of negative long-term outcomes which are associated with running away, including homelessness, social exclusion and involvement in prostitution, together with a potential range of other factors such as ill-health and poor life prospects suggested by US research.

2 e.g., Greene and Ringwalt, 1998; Ensign and Santelli, 1998

3 e.g., Greene, Ennett and Ringwalt, 1999

4 e.g., Booth et al, 1999; Dangelo et al, 1994; Busen and Beech, 1997

5 e.g., Pennbridge, Mackenzie and Swofford, 1991; Molnar et al, 1998; Adlaf and Zdanowicz, 1999

6 e.g., Ensign and Santelli, 1998; Pennbridge, Mackenzie and Swofford, 1991; Unger et al, 1997

7 e.g., Pennbridge, Mackenzie and Swofford, 1991; Ensign and Santelli, 1998; Unger et al, 1997

3

REFUGES

Introduction

This chapter looks at refuges run under Section 51 of the Children Act 1989. In total, there have been five such refuges in operation since 1991 (see the Introduction for more details). The focus here is mainly on two of these refuges – Leeds Safe House and the Porth Project (which operated in Newport, South Wales) – and the chapter also incorporates some learning from the Southside Refuge in Bournemouth.

Case studies

CASE STUDY 1

Leeds Safe House   *The Children's Society*

Leeds Safe House started providing accommodation for young people in February 1991. It was the third refuge to be set up in the UK. For the first eight months of its operation the project technically worked outside the law, until the introduction in October 1991 of the Children Act 1989 made such refuges legal for the first time (see Chapter 1 for details). Two years later the refuge was one of the first in the country to be given a certificate under Section 51 of that Act. The project operated for nearly ten years, closing in October 2000 for financial reasons, as described in Chapter 1.

Leeds Safe House was based at a confidential address. The accommodation was a large four-storey house in a residential area of Leeds, which was adapted to provided accommodation for six to eight young people (some in shared rooms), a living room and kitchen, together with offices, meeting rooms and a sleep-in room for staff. The refuge was staffed 24 hours a day, and there was a minimum of two workers on duty at any one time.

The key elements of the project's practice were a 'young-person-centred approach' and an emphasis on 'advocacy' work, both of which are discussed further in Chapter 8.

CASE STUDY 2

The Porth Project   *The Children's Society*

The Porth Project, which offered refuge in Newport, South Wales from 1993 to 1999, had many features in common with Leeds Safe House, including its referral process and its methods and approaches to working with young people.

The distinctive aspect of the Porth Project, compared with the other four refuges that have so far operated in the UK, is that it provided accommodation for young people through a pool of foster carers rather than through a central residential unit. Refuge carers were recruited specifically to provide this service, and were subject both to approval as foster carers by The Children's Society and to certification as a refuge under Section 51 by the Welsh Office. Young people stayed at the refuge carers' homes except for during office hours on weekdays, when they were brought to a project base where project staff would work with them on the issues that had caused them to run away, as discussed for Leeds Safe House above.

Unfortunately, it seems that the resources required to operate this model were initially under-estimated and the project experienced considerable difficulties in maintaining an adequate pool of refuge carers. The model was shown to be practically effective at times, but ultimately the lack of resources led to a sporadic level of service and eventually the project was closed and redeveloped in Cardiff as Two-Way Street – a drop-in centre and street-work-based model.

Description of work

Target group

Both refuges under discussion in this chapter worked with young people under the age of 16 who had run away or been forced to leave home and were currently at risk. The Porth Project additionally worked with young people over the age of 16 who were running away from substitute care. At Leeds Safe House, as the work developed, the criteria for admission to refuge became slightly more restrictive. Emphasis was placed on accommodating young people who would be at risk if they returned to the place from which they had run away. In the case of young people from substitute care, procedures were put into place to ensure that, in most instances, a safe place was available within the care system rather than through refuge. This latter development was due to high levels of usage and associated difficulties that the project encountered in providing refuge for young people running away from children's homes:

> 'One of the factors that led to refuge being clogged up, if you like, was the high number of re-referrals from the same young people and many of those came from young people running away from local authority care, particularly children's homes.'

Methods of contact

Due to the confidential location of the two refuges, referrals were only taken by telephone, directly from young people or through agencies and other sources with young people's active participation. A project worker (or two project workers in the case of the Porth Project) would then go out to meet the young person in a car, have an initial discussion about the service on offer and, where appropriate, take the young person into refuge. The police were informed of the young person's arrival, and they in turn informed the young person's parent(s) or carers that the young person was in refuge at a confidential location. This was followed up by a letter from the project to the parents/carers.

Models of service delivery

One aspect of service delivery in refuges is the provision of shelter, safety, food and other practical assistance to young people. Beyond this immediate practical support, the work of the projects would initially focus on developing an understanding of the issues which had caused the young person to run away, and drawing up an action plan with the young person to work on the issues they were facing. This would then be followed up by 'advocacy' work with parents, carers or professionals as appropriate. Ultimately the aim was usually either for the young person to return to the place from which they had run away, or to find a suitable alternative place to live (e.g., substitute care or relatives).

Under Section 51 of the Children Act 1989, young people could remain at the refuge for a continuous stay of up to 14 nights and for a maximum of 21 nights in any three-month period, although at Leeds this latter rule was extended by the project to a six-month period in order to limit repeat usage and ensure that the service was accessible to a range of young people (see Discussion below).

Both projects adopted a crisis intervention model and did only a limited amount of follow-up work with young people. Again, some of the issues arising from this approach are discussed below.

Discussion

Contributors who worked in refuges tended to be more self-critical than those working in other settings. There was a great deal of reflection on the difficulties involved in refuge provision. This means there is a risk, in presenting these views of contributors, of painting a predominantly negative picture of the potential for refuges to work effectively with young people who run away.

Therefore, before embarking on a critical appraisal of some of the issues and difficulties experienced by the two projects under discussion, it is worth emphasising the successes of both projects in providing a safety net for young people who run away.

The provision of a safety net

Refuge offers an instantly accessible and tangible service to young people which can prevent their exposure to the difficulties and risks of spending time 'on the streets', while helping them to try to resolve the issues that led to them running away in the first place. Both projects worked with substantial numbers of young people during their operation (Leeds Safe House provided almost 2,000 stays for over 1,000 young people in nine-and-a-half years and the Porth Project accommodated 109 young people over a six-year period).

Leeds Safe House was registered as a children's home as part of the requirements for certification under Section 51 of the Children Act. It subsequently received twice-yearly inspections by the Social Services Inspectorate and achieved increasingly complimentary inspection reports with regard to its standards of practice in working with young people. In this sense the project was a highly successful example of the potential of providing emergency accommodation for young people who run away.

There seems little doubt in most contributors' minds that the provision of accommodation/refuge is a valuable option to have available when working with young people who run away. What is at issue is the nature of this provision and the extent to which it is an appropriate universal service for these young people.

Operational issues

For both the Leeds Safe House and the Porth Project, the effort entailed in maintaining a 24-hour emergency resource for young people was a major issue. In the case of Leeds it was necessary to maintain a large bank of sessional workers in order to ensure cover for annual leave and for unexpected absences of project staff for sickness and other reasons. Although the project hardly ever had to shut its doors due to staff shortages in the nine years of its existence, the effort of covering the rota took up a considerable amount of management time. The large staff team also placed high line management and supervisory demands on Senior Project Workers.

In the case of the Porth Project, the recruitment and maintenance of a sufficient bank of refuge carers took up considerable resources. The whole process of recruiting a new refuge carer, including approval as a foster carer and certification under Section 51, took at least six months, and usually longer. With a relatively small staff team, and some turnover of foster carers, it proved difficult for the project to maintain a continuous service for young people. At times there were insufficient staff to cover the rota and at other times there were insufficient foster carers to offer refuge for young people.

In addition, for both projects, the continuous, unpredictable and inherently risky nature of the work meant that an out-of-hours on-call rota had to be drawn up for senior staff to support staff and refuge carers. This again had a substantial impact on managers, who sometimes experienced a feeling of being constantly at work for lengthy periods.

Some of the issues for managers of projects working with young people who run away are discussed further in Chapter 11.

A comparison of the strengths and weakness of centralised and dispersed models of refuge

Part of the initial rationale for the Porth Project appears to have been the expectation that it would provide a cost-effective alternative to the centralised refuge model, which might be viable outside major cities where the smaller population base would mean a lower demand for refuge services. Ultimately this does not seem to have been the case. The project had a substantially smaller budget latterly (in the region of £350,000) than Leeds Safe House but was beset by difficulties in terms of simultaneously staffing the project on a 24-hour basis and recruiting and supporting refuge carers. This meant that the project was only sporadically able to provide a full service to young people. It may be that other models of dispersed refuge would work out cheaper, but in the absence of current evidence of substantial financial differences it is interesting to explore the other relative strengths and weaknesses of the two models.

The centralised refuge model is arguably more straightforward to run. Everything takes place at one location, and this avoids some of the complications of the dispersed model, such as the need to ferry young people back and forth to a project base in the daytime to do focused work, and the need to support a separate pool of dedicated carers. For young people a single location provision may give a greater sense of consistency during a period of insecurity and uncertainty.

On the other hand, in a centralised model the fact that young people are living together raises other issues. One of these concerns the drain on staff resources in dealing with group dynamics:

> *'The dynamics could change so quickly and I think residential-based refuge is not always right for all young people... I think you've got to be fairly bold about establishing what you are going to focus on. You can decide that as a refuge you can't accommodate young people with a drugs habit, because to do so may be detrimental to the safety of other young people using the refuge – but having done that, are you then turning away very needy young people?'*

Another potential drawback relates to the possible diversity of young people using a refuge, and the risk that young people might be introduced to new and risky activities by other young people:

> *'The make-up of the young people you have within any one building... it's the very nature of the work that young people using refuge can be a combination of ages, gender, experiences, family backgrounds; whether it's the first time that they've run away or whether they've been on the streets for three months or more. It's such a huge variety of differences... you have no control over how you manage the intake of that. You don't know the young people, you don't have any of their backgrounds. [With other residential services] you would know what were the individual needs and requirements of the young person, what their likes and dislikes were, whether you needed to be aware of any particular issues in staffing – those sorts of things – whereas in refuge you don't have any of that.'*

However, this risk posed by the differences between young people might be counterbalanced by the potential for mutually supportive relationships between young people with common experiences.

In addition to avoiding some of the above problems of communal living, a dispersed model has other potential strengths. It makes a clear distinction between the caring role of refuge carers and the problem-solving role of project workers. Thus project workers do not have to spend time catering for young people's physical and practical needs, while young people can experience a consistency of care within a community-based environment, which usually can be a positive aspect (although a placement within a family home might not suit all young people who run away).

One of the key drawbacks of the dispersed model is the complexities introduced by the need to recruit, support and manage a dispersed group of foster carers. At the Porth Project this was found to be a resource-intensive aspect of running the service. A large amount of time was invested in the process of approving and certificating foster carers, and a number of structures were put in place, including a dedicated support worker, individual supervision and group sessions, to ensure that the carers were adequately supported. These considerations need to be carefully weighed against some of the evident advantages of the dispersed model already mentioned.

The need for refuge as opposed to emergency accommodation

There is a fair degree of consensus among contributors that while many young people who run away are in need of emergency accommodation, relatively few are being actively pursued and therefore in need of 'refuge' in the sense of a confidential location. To an extent, then, it seems that a more open form of accommodation might be suitable for most young people:

> 'I think it was something that in the early stages we were, perhaps, over-protective of; the staff were very protective of the location... maybe again that's because we weren't sure what the reaction was going to be, and the idea of young people under 16 being away from home without their parents' permission – the perception was that their parents or carers would come looking for them and therefore they needed to be hidden. I think the reality of it has been... maybe half-a-dozen occasions where young people have been actively pursued, one where I think a parent did actually knock on the door and come running through the house and chase them out of the other end, and occasions where we got people waiting outside the front and back of the house, looking for particular young people. I think those cases are fairly extreme. In the majority of cases I think that, sadly, a lot of the parents and carers hadn't even reported them missing, so they weren't that interested in where they were or actively pursuing them to get them back.'

However, some contributors felt that the whole experience and safety of refuge provision was viewed as very important by many of the young people with whom they had worked:

> 'What it did give though, I think – and [I don't know] whether you'd get that without the notion of it being at a confidential location – is the trust from the young people, that when you said "nobody will come here and take you away", they believed that. Part of that belief was instilled by the fact that its location wasn't disclosed to anybody, and I think that if you tried to get that same level of trust by just saying "look, they know where we are but we won't let them in", there's a big difference there... I think it's about demonstrating that what you say is what you mean. So I think giving young people the message is an important aspect.'

Refuge provision therefore may have benefits that are less tangible, and which might not exist in a more functional accommodation-based model:

> 'I think it's really powerful symbolically that you take a young person in. You take them in physically, and by taking them in physically you take them in emotionally. Especially as young people are particularly vulnerable when they're in crisis. You remember it, don't you, people who were there for you when you were in real trouble.'

A related question is whether refuge or other accommodation for young people under 16 who run away has to be provided within the framework of Section 51. That framework was specifically designed to protect refuge projects from prosecution for 'harbouring' a young runaway. The experience of refuge staff has been that in most cases parents and carers do not object to young people being accommodated in refuge. It is therefore possible for a project to provide accommodation for a young person with parental consent, and thus without recourse to the provisions of Section 51. The Home & Away Project in London (discussed in more detail in Chapter 6) occasionally accommodates young people on this basis with emergency foster carers for up to three nights. There are plans for the South Coast Runaways Initiative (also discussed in Chapter 6) to accommodate young people in supported bed-and-breakfast accommodation for a few nights in a similar manner:

> 'When I first heard that [we might have to seek parental consent for refuge] I was quite cynical and sceptical and thought, that won't work. Actually, having done a year's work, of the people that I have identified that would have fitted the criteria for refuge and would have needed it – we're only talking small amounts. Of those 48, 13 would have benefited I think from a refuge; parental consent wouldn't have been a problem, I don't think. And, in fact, I think in many cases parents would have welcomed the fact that there was somewhere safe for their sons or daughters to go while we tried to sort out where to go next.'

Nevertheless, Section 51 remains an important provision for young people who are in need of a safe place to stay for a short period, in cases where there is a risk that parents, carers or other people might pursue them or attempt to force them to return to a situation from which they had run away.

Several contributors commented on the unusual nature of working in a confidential refuge and the effects that this could have on the staff team. In both Leeds and Newport, it was felt that the protected location had at times contributed to a tendency towards insularity. This tendency was perhaps also exacerbated by the lack of a financial relationship with other agencies. There seems to have been little networking with other agencies, with detrimental effects for both the staff (in terms of a narrow perspective) and the young people (in terms of missed opportunities for referral to other suitable services). This is an aspect of refuge work which project managers may need to make conscious efforts to counteract.

The strengths and weaknesses of providing accommodation for young people who run away

One of the key problems of providing accommodation that contributors highlighted is the fact that it can slow down the responsiveness of other agencies. In extreme circumstances, the fact that a young person was accommodated safely in a refuge diminished their priority in the eyes of statutory services, which consequently began to respond only when the 14-day maximum time limit approached.

On occasions when refuge was not available the response could be much quicker. This view was reinforced by contributors who had worked both in refuge and street-work projects; they felt that the latter projects were often able to exert more pressure on statutory services due to the fact that they did not have accommodation to offer. This apparent weakness of refuge projects is particularly relevant in circumstances where the young person is already accommodated by the local authority, or where admission into substitute care seems an appropriate option.

Additionally, some contributors expressed concern that, at times, refuges could be used as an extension of the substitute care system to cover gaps in emergency statutory provision. This seemed to have happened gradually at the Southside Refuge, which was initially set up with the support of the local authority and the police. As the project became established within the local network, there was some drift away from the original conception of refuge provision. The project continued to provide a valuable breathing space for young people, but did not always do this in the way that had been originally intended:

> 'Over time it became part of the local system, which I don't think we had intended when we set it up. So what was happening was that for the 16- and 17-year-olds we were seen as an emergency place [where] those young people could go, and with the under-16s we had become part of the emergency system used by social services. The night duty team were regularly "placing" (not in the legal sense) young people with us who were having rows in the night, as a kind of cooling-off period. So I think in terms of the core work that we had set ourselves up to do, there were only about 15 young people a year who fitted the original brief.'

This move away from the original aims ultimately led to the closure of the refuge and the development of a family intervention service which has been successful in working with broadly the same group of young people using a different model (see also Chapter 7).

There are also some concerns about the suitability of refuge as a service for some young people from minority ethnic groups. As discussed in Chapter 10, the use of refuge can have major repercussions for some young people and it may be that other interventions which are specifically geared to particular cultural contexts will have more positive long-term outcomes.

In contrast to the above points, one of the great strengths of the refuge model is the breathing space for young people and families alike offered by refuges, and the opportunity to cool off and take stock of a situation within relative safety. Some contributors felt that the security of 24-hour provision also increased the potential for young people to 'open up' to staff, including making fresh disclosures of abuse.

However, there was a fairly unanimous opinion among contributors that most young people did not usually need to take the 14 days allowed in law:

> 'Providing accommodation for young people for up to a fortnight doesn't work. Three or four nights I think is about the limit. If you go past there, then it's just not worth it.'

It was felt that a stay away from home of this length of time could create a rift between young people and their family:

> 'One of the pitfalls of just having the refuge as we had it was that even over a 14-day period it could develop too much of a rift with the family. The majority of times the young person had to go back to the family, and there was work done with the family, but it wasn't the priority. It sort of added to the problems... I had quite a lot of worries about it. Did it create a greater rift and did we do enough to support the family to support the young person?'

For these reasons, most contributors saw a period of three or four days as sufficient to negotiate a return home in the large majority of situations.

Another potential problem with accommodation-based projects is that young people may seek to be accommodated in order to obtain other services offered by the project (such as information, problem-solving and advocacy) or because they valued the way in which the project worked:

> *'I think that some young people came into refuge inappropriately because they actually needed to come back to people they knew, and that that ended up sometimes being less helpful to them in terms of resolving their difficulties at home... the emotional needs of the young people we were working with [needed] to be met and they [needed] to be met in an open, agreed way that [was] appropriate, rather than veiled behind other things.'*

Although in later years, both Leeds Safe House and the Porth Project attempted to offer services to young people irrespective of whether they came into refuge, it is still true of both projects that the large majority of staff resources were devoted to working with young people in refuge. As shown in Chapter 2, research suggests that around two-thirds of young people who run away sleep at the houses of relatives or friends while away from home. There is clearly a danger of projects accommodating young people who have no need of accommodation, resulting in wasted resources and potentially negative side-effects. This suggests that refuge should be provided as one component of an integrated service for young people who run away, a point that is picked up in later chapters of the report.

An associated problem for both projects was that they did relatively little follow-on work with young people after they had left refuge. This was partly due to the lack of resources, and partly out of a desire to avoid long-term involvement with the young people and the dependency that this might create. The limited amount of follow-on work could, however, sometimes result in a cyclical pattern of refuge usage by young people who were arguably in need of a long-term involvement. This confounded the projects' desires to limit the length of involvement and also, perhaps more worryingly, led to disjointed work which failed to tackle the complex issues that caused these young people to run away repeatedly.

Additionally, the fact that refuge projects, by necessity, have a structured approach to working with young people, including a large number of rules and expectations of behaviour, may limit their attractiveness to some young people. It might even completely put off some of the more detached young people who have become used to less obviously restrictive ways of living.

In the early days of refuge provision there were fears that providing refuge within a particular geographical area might 'encourage' young people to run away in that area, once they knew that there was somewhere to go. There is no evidence that, in general, these fears have been borne out in terms of frivolous or inappropriate use of refuge, although there were some issues at Leeds Safe House about high usage by young people in substitute care, as noted earlier. However, for some young people, it may be that the existence of a refuge in the locality provides a sense of security which enables them to escape from an abusive situation.

Developmental issues

A particular issue to be aware of when initiating projects that provide accommodation for young people who run away is the long lead-in time involved in setting up the service. The complexities of identifying appropriate premises, recruiting staff and/or refuge carers, and obtaining the necessary inspections and certifications to work under Section 51 of the Children Act mean that the period from starting the project to beginning work with young people can be anything from one to two years. This has major resource implications and there is a need to phase the recruitment and employment of staff carefully. At Leeds Safe House it was 18 months from the employment of the project leader before the first young person was accommodated, and this was at a time when it was not necessary to obtain legal approval for refuge. The Porth Project experienced unexpected delays due to legal issues and this meant that staff and carers who had already been recruited were left in limbo for several months. Similarly, Checkpoint's recent efforts to set up a flexible refuge in Torquay (discussed in Chapter 6) have encountered legal problems, and sessional workers who were recruited to do this work have now moved on.

Key points

- Refuges have proved a successful model in providing a safety net for young people who run away and who might otherwise have ended up on the streets or sleeping rough.

- Independent inspection has validated the refuge model and verified the potential for providing high-quality emergency accommodation for young people in this target group.

- The refuge model can be the platform for an effective short-term intervention to help young people to resolve the difficulties that led to them run away, and can often facilitate a speedy return to the place from which they ran away.

- The models of refuge which have been utilised to date have been relatively costly. They are also highly resource-intensive in terms of staffing and this can have an impact on the senior staff who are responsible for supervising and supporting staff, and maintaining a continuous service.

- There may be less difference between the costs of the centralised and dispersed models than might be imagined. The models have counterbalancing strengths and weaknesses in other respects, concerning practical operational issues and benefits for young people.

- It appears that there is a relatively small need for a confidential refuge among young people who run away. However, the sense of security provided by refuges may be of benefit to a larger number of young people. Refuge managers need to be alert to the risks of insularity which seem to be inherent in refuge provision.

- In general, contributors felt that it was preferable in most cases to limit the length of time that young people spent in refuge to much less than the 14 nights allowed in law.

- There is a tendency towards lack of flexibility in the refuge model, but it may be particularly suitable for a particular sub-group of the overall population of young people who run away. These are young people who would otherwise have nowhere safe to sleep, for whom a quick return home is relatively likely, who are not engaged in a repetitive cycle of running away, and have not experienced lengthy periods of detachment or living on the streets.

■ It seems to be legally acceptable, with parental consent, to accommodate young people under the age of 16 who run away, without recourse to Section 51 of the Children Act. This potentially opens up more flexible forms of emergency accommodation for young people.

■ The crisis intervention model usually employed by refuges can run into problems with young people who run away repeatedly. There is a need to consider the most effective ways of meeting these young people's longer-term needs, as there is a danger of cyclical use of refuge.

4

STREET WORK

Introduction

This chapter focuses on the work of two projects which pioneered detached work with young people under 18 on the streets in major city centres – Youth Link in Birmingham and Safe in the City in Manchester. Both these projects have been carrying out work on the streets with young people in conjunction with a range of other services (including drop-in services and telephone lines) for the past decade.

Case studies

CASE STUDY 1

Youth Link, Birmingham   *The Children's Society*

Youth Link was the first project working with young people running away to be opened outside London by The Children's Society, being one of a number of projects set up to respond to the developing awareness of the incidence of young people from around the country ending up on the streets in London.

The project opened in 1988, initially providing detached street work and drop-in services for young people on the streets in Birmingham city centre. Where appropriate, the project would advocate on young people's behalf. This advocacy work can be done with young people either on the street, or in the drop-in centre.

In recent years the project has also developed other services. It has run a missing persons scheme, as briefly discussed in Chapter 5, and has also developed a website aimed at young people (see Chapter 7).

CASE STUDY 2

Safe in the City, Manchester   *The Children's Society*

Safe in the City opened in 1989 and was initially conceived rather differently from Youth Link. Three distinct services were envisaged: street work, advocacy and refuge. However, the idea of setting up a refuge was later abandoned, and it became apparent also that the model of advocacy envisaged would not be particularly suitable for the young people with whom the project was working, as discussed later in this chapter.

The project therefore concentrated its efforts on the detached street work, and at some points in its existence has also offered some drop-in facilities to young people. The model of operation is broadly the same as described for Youth Link above.

continued overleaf

> **CASE STUDY 2 *continued***
>
> Safe in the City has also diversified its services over the last few years. The project has split into three teams: one working specifically with black young people, one working with young people who are being sexually exploited and one generic street-work team which has widened its brief to cover areas outside Manchester city centre. The project has undertaken preventive work in children's homes (see Chapter 7) and is also developing a missing persons scheme aimed at making contact with missing young people while they are away from home.

Description of work

Target group

Both projects work primarily with under-18-year-olds who spend time on the streets within the city centre. This includes young people who are literally living on the streets, young people who have temporary accommodation but use the streets as part of their survival strategies, and other young people who have stable or semi-stable accommodation but sporadically spend time on the streets. There is some practical difficulty in maintaining an upper age limit, partly because people do not always divulge their age, and partly because an overly rigid approach could reduce the project's credibility.

Methods of contact

The projects make contact with young people either through an active approach to a young person by a project worker or through the young person approaching the worker. The latter often occurs through word-of-mouth recommendation from other young people on the streets, which is dependent on the extent to which the project has been able to establish its credibility amongst the community of people living on the streets.

Models of service delivery

The two projects' model of street-work delivery has remained basically unaltered since its beginning. Project workers operate in pairs, usually at set times, in and around the city centre where young people are known to spend time. On initial contact with young people the workers explain what the project offers, and they are able to offer practical and emotional support and information if the young person wants this. They also publicise the existence of the drop-in service.

The Youth Link drop-in model has varied somewhat over time, as discussed later in this chapter, but is intended as a place to carry out focused pieces of work with young people, rather than to act as an informal place where young people can congregate. The drop-in also offers practical facilities, such as showers and a washing machine. Safe in the City offers similar centre-based work and facilities.

The ongoing work with young people on the streets at both projects can take a variety of forms and is primarily young person led. It includes elements of information-giving, harm minimisation, practical support and the possibility of advocacy in certain circumstances.

Discussion

One of the great achievements of the two projects described in the preceding pages has been their ability to engage with young people who have become marginalised from mainstream society.

This success aside, contributors' comments regarding learning from street work focused on four broad areas: environmental factors, the nature and extent to which it is possible to undertake work on the streets, the concept of crisis intervention when doing street work, and issues of diversity. These four areas are explored in detail in the remainder of this chapter. The reader is also referred to the discussion in Chapter 11 on personal safety issues for workers doing detached street work.

The ability to engage with detached young people

Research and practice experience have shown that young people who run away and spend time on the streets in city centres often have a specific set of characteristics and experiences which distinguish them from other young runaways. They are likely to have come from particularly abusive or damaging backgrounds; to have run away a number of times and/or spent long continuous periods away from home; and to have spent time living in substitute care. In many cases, these experiences will have led them to be mistrustful of adults, including social welfare professionals (Stein, Rees and Frost, 1994).

Environmental factors

Environmental factors are particularly relevant to detached street work in two ways. First, unlike in services based within buildings, street workers are working in an environment over which they have little or no control:

'We don't own the streets, we have very little say on the street – we're visitors.'

This lack of control may put workers at some risk and it has been necessary to develop good strategies for maximising personal safety, as discussed in Chapter 11, but it also has other implications.

Workers are not invited onto the streets and this increases the need for sensitive handling of the process of making contact with young people. Young people may be wary of professionals or adults on the streets and will also have their own priorities (including carving out a survival strategy) upon which street workers may impinge by their presence. On the other hand, there is a need to be active in making initial contact with young people in order to make them aware of what the project can offer them. Both projects have developed strategies for approaching young people sensitively.

It is also vital that workers establish a workable relationship with other people in the 'street community'. This might include homeless adults, the owners of night-clubs and all-night cafés, other outreach workers, and so on. A street-work project needs to establish a certain amount of credibility within this community in order to be successful. If this is achieved, many young people will be referred to, or introduced to, the street workers by other people on the streets. This need for credibility also raises problematic issues, however. A clear confidentiality policy is an essential prerequisite for any project working with young people who run away (see Chapter 8). But for street work, the issue of confidentiality has an added dimension in that breaches of confidentiality in relation to individual young people can jeopardise the status of the whole project. If the project gains a reputation of not being worthy of trust it can lose its ability to engage with young people.

The second way in which environmental factors are crucial to street work is that the environment can change in unexpected ways over time, again totally outside the control of the project. For example, Manchester city centre has undergone fundamental changes over the last decade. Areas which were quite run down have been modernised and moved up-market, closed-circuit surveillance has increased, and policing strategies have varied. All these changes have had implications for street culture and, consequently, for the work of Safe in the City. At times, the changes have meant that there have been few young people to work with.

Street-work projects therefore need in-built flexibility in order to deal with a changing environment. It is also probably true to say that city-centre-based street-work projects working with young people who run away need, to a far greater extent than the other kinds of services discussed in this report, to be designed for a particular local context. Each city will have its own characteristics in terms of street culture, and models of practice which are effective in one location will not necessarily be transferable to another.

The nature and extent of work on the street

As originally envisaged, the street work at both projects was seen as a form of outreach work: a means by which the project would make contact with young people who would then gain access to other services, such as advocacy and (in the case of Safe in the City) refuge. One of the key learning points for both projects has been the fact that workers have been able to engage actively with young people on the streets to a greater extent than was originally anticipated. In Youth Link this has led to a reassessment of the place of street work within the range of services the project offers:

> 'What we recognised was that there was a large group of young people who don't want to use the drop-in [centre] or the core time, and they actually want to have the work done with them out on the streets. So a further development of the detached work has actually been daytime detached work, which has come in in the last three years, and again we try very hard to make sure that we do maintain at least two or three of those a week.'

In Manchester, it also became clear that many of the young people would be unlikely to use a refuge facility even if the project set one up, and also that the notion of advocacy was not always particularly attractive to them.

The reasons for the above points related to the nature of young people's existence on the streets. Young people develop survival strategies involving various legitimate (and illegitimate) ways of earning money or obtaining food and basic items, and they often rely on a network of friends and acquaintances for temporary accommodation. While this existence can be stressful and at times dangerous, it is often seen by the young people as preferable to returning to the places from which they have run away. Coupled with this, young people on the streets have often developed a deep-seated mistrust of professionals and their interventions, founded on disappointments and negative experiences in the past. They are therefore reluctant to take the leap of faith that using a refuge or advocacy service would require of them. Because of their survival strategies their time horizons are also quite short – often focusing on where the next meal is coming from, or where they might sleep that night. Some young people do not envisage being alive in a year's time and, in the experience of contributors, this is not a completely unfounded fear. Others are simply biding their time until they become 16, when they imagine (often unrealistically) that they will be able to secure independent accommodation.

All these factors militate against the likelihood of engagement with professionals and agencies in order to try to find alternative solutions to their current situation. However, both projects have gradually developed ways of working with young people within the street environment. This has been partly facilitated by mobile phone technology. Workers no longer need to take a young person to a central base to undertake advocacy work:

> *'At one point in the history of Youth Link, the only way a young person could be worked with is if they came into the project. Even on the late evening sessions it would be, "Come into the project tomorrow and we'll sort it out for you." Whereas now young people will be given the choice. One of the developments is having the technology of a mobile phone which means that if a young person wants to sort out a meeting, or benefits, or social services appointment, or whatever, we can actually do it there and then during the daytime, whip the phone out and off we go. It also means that we are freer to go and accompany young people to significant meetings for support.'*

This means that the projects can respond immediately to the issues that young people raise, and this has become an important factor in the project's success in engaging with some of the most mistrustful young people:

> *'I think we end up working with almost more extremes [i.e., young people in more extreme situations]. I think a lot of young people can be a bit suspicious... if your instant response is "We can help you but you need to come down to the building", they think, "What's going on?" whereas if we say, "We can help you, would you like us to do it now, or we could meet up tomorrow, somewhere that you've decided", I think that allows us to work with some of the more "suspicious of agency" type young people. I think the feeling is that "I'll have to do this, this and this to get a service", and what we really strongly try and promote now is that you don't actually have to do anything to get our service other than say, "Could you help me?"'*

Crisis intervention with young people on the streets

The original application of the notion of crisis intervention to young people who run away was in terms of understanding the factors that led to them running away from their home. It was assumed that the running away incident itself was fairly short-lived and was part of this crisis. The role of projects working in this field was therefore seen as using the opportunity presented by the crisis to resolve key issues in young people's lives at the same time as facilitating a return home. For the young people who are worked with by street-work projects this model does not fit particularly well. They may not see themselves as currently being in crisis; they may in fact have a fairly stable set of survival strategies, and they will probably not see the return to the place from which they ran away as particularly desirable. The idea of offering crisis-intervention work on the basis described above does not therefore fit in with the realities of these young people's lives.

However, a different application of the crisis intervention model has emerged which can guide the model of work undertaken on the streets. To a certain extent, the aims of street-work projects can be seen as establishing and maintaining a basic relationship or credibility with young people. At one level this relationship can form the basis of work aimed at harm reduction. If the relationship can be achieved at that point, when there is a breakdown in the young people's established survival strategies or an event that disturbs the flimsy stability of their lives on the streets, the project may be in a position to intervene in this crisis and enable the young person to move off the streets. Thus street work can be seen as having two aims in terms of direct work with young people: ongoing harm minimisation (e.g., in relation to risky behaviour such as substance misuse and criminal activity), and occasional crisis intervention when the opportunity presents itself. (A third aim of street work is to facilitate young people's access to other service provision.)

This bare outline of the street-work model identifies a key source of stress for project workers. They will often have to walk away from young people on the streets in risky situations because the young person does not want any further intervention. It also means that, when a crisis does arise for a young person, the workers may have a considerable amount of emotional investment in achieving a change in the young person's life. If this proves impossible it can be particularly demoralising for project staff.

Street work and diversity

Research indicates that street work undertaken in the centres of large cities tends to engage with a very specific sub-group of young people who run away. These are young people who have become detached, often with extensive experience of living in substitute care, and they are predominantly white (Stein, Rees and Frost, 1994). The reasons for the lack of black young people on the streets have been explored in a recent research study (Safe on the Streets Research Team, 1999) which highlighted the experiences of racism on the streets as a key factor, and indicated that black and Asian young people are less likely than white young people to sleep rough and more likely to rely on informal support within their communities when they are away from home. These findings are supported by a recent research study (not yet published) of black young people running away, which has been conducted in Manchester by Safe in the City:

> 'Black young people do not find Manchester city centre a safe place. So in terms of the way we operate, city centre street work was not necessarily going to meet their needs. From my own personal experience, I've only met one or two [black young people] in the whole of the time I was doing street work.'

This is one of the factors that led Safe in the City to set up a black young people's team, the early work of which is described in Chapter 10.

The limitations of city-centre street work may be more widespread than this, however. Research also indicates that young people running away from families are unlikely to go outside their local area, and there is very little evidence of their migrating to the centres of large cities (several research studies, including Rees, 1993; Safe on the Streets Research Team, 1999). This means that street work may ultimately engage predominantly with very specific sub-groups of young people who run away, such as young people running away from the substitute care system, young people who have run away from families and have become 'detached', and young people who are being sexually exploited. Therefore it may well be that the kinds of community-based interventions targeted at black young people being devised and piloted by Safe in the City described in Chapter 10 are also applicable to working with detached young white people running away from home and staying within their communities.

Key points

- The street-work model has proved highly successful at engaging with young people who have become detached from mainstream society and may be particularly mistrustful of adults.

- Successful street work requires a careful engagement with the street environment, which is largely beyond the control of the project, and thoughtful and sensitive methods of making contact with young people within this environment.

- The street environment can change over time, and therefore street-work projects also need to be flexible in order to cope with a shifting basis for their work.

- Street work with young runaways was originally seen as an outreach activity, but methods of carrying out significant pieces of work in the street environment have gradually been developed.

- However, many young people on the streets will not want to move off the streets and so projects need to focus on harm minimisation and on patiently developing a long-term relationship with young people, so that if they encounter a crisis and do wish to move off the streets, they will feel able to trust the project.

- City-centre-based street work will not reach all groups of detached young people who run away. In particular, it is unlikely to reach black young people, and may also tend to be focused more on young people running away from substitute care than those from families. There is therefore a need to pilot alternative forms of detached work.

5

MISSING PERSONS SCHEMES

Introduction

This chapter focuses on a number of schemes which receive all or a large proportion of their referrals as a result of young people being reported as missing to the police. This is a relatively new area of service provision for young people who run away.

Police receive reports of people of all ages who are missing from home, usually from relatives or carers of the missing person. It is standard working practice for the police to follow up on these reports and to visit the person if they return home. However, in relation to young people, it became clear from early research studies into running away (e.g., Rees, 1993) that the police may not be the best-placed agency to offer such a service. Young people often view the police with mistrust and are unwilling to engage with them. It was also clear from research that many young people return home without anyone having explored the reasons why they ran away. Consequently, it has been the recommendation of several research reports that non-statutory agencies attempt to talk to young people reported missing when they return home, with a view to offering a listening ear, providing advice and information, and potentially engaging with them, where appropriate, to seek solutions to the issues that led to them running away.

The first scheme of this kind was probably a pilot project carried out by Leeds Safe House in 1996. This chapter draws on the work of five current schemes which can be categorised as being wholly or partly missing persons schemes, two run by Barnardo's in Bradford and Kirklees in West Yorkshire, two run by The Children's Society in Leeds and Birmingham, and one run by the ASTRA Project in Gloucester. There are also schemes currently in operation in the Midlands run by Barnardo's, and in Manchester and London run by The Children's Society. Moreover, there are several other schemes in the pipeline, including in Cardiff, Torquay and Glasgow. Missing persons schemes have therefore become a key model of intervention with young people who run away.

Apart from having the same source of referrals, all the projects considered in this chapter have something in common in terms of their means of initially engaging with young people. In contrast to the refuge and centre-based projects, they actively go into the community in order to make contact with young people who have run away or may be at risk of running away, visiting them in their homes and at other locations, such as schools. This method of contact has certain strengths but also raises a number of issues, which will be discussed later in the chapter.

Case studies

CASE STUDY 1

ASTRA   *Independent*

The ASTRA (Alternative Solutions to Running Away) Project was set up by a consortium of local statutory and voluntary agencies in Gloucester in 1998. The scheme originated in concerns noted by the police about missing young people, which were emphasised by the Fred and Rosemary West case.

ASTRA works with young people under 18 in the Gloucester area (including young people in substitute care). The project takes referrals from a range of sources (including agencies, parents and young people themselves), and so is not exclusively a missing persons scheme. However, the most common source of referrals to the project stems from police missing persons reports, and a key intended outcome of the project's work is to reduce the repeat incidence of young people being reported as missing to the police. The project receives details of young people who have run away, and makes direct contact with them when they return home.

CASE STUDY 2

Bradford Young Missing Persons Scheme   *Barnardo's*

This project developed from within Barnardo's Streets and Lanes Project in Bradford, which focuses on girls and young women at risk of being, or who are being, abused through prostitution. The early learning from this latter project had been that there was a connection between young women being sexually exploited and their running away. In many cases, the 'grooming' process through which sexual exploitation took place was started while young women were missing from home. Consequently, the multi-agency steering group supported the creating of a pilot project aimed at young women reported as missing. The idea was that contact would be made with young women in order to assess their risk of becoming involved in sexual exploitation, and to work with them or refer them on to the main scheme where appropriate.

The pilot was run in one area of Bradford and was perceived to have been a success. As a result, Barnardo's made a successful application to the Department of Health for joint funding of an ongoing scheme. The resulting project expanded its activities to cover all areas of Bradford.

More recently, the project has obtained Quality Protects funding to provide independent interviews for young people who run away from substitute care. This development will be accompanied by a local protocol on dealing with running away from care, which the project has been instrumental in drawing up, together with the police and social services.

Description of work

Target groups

The projects work with slightly different target groups of young people. The ASTRA Project works with young people who have been reported missing to the police more than twice plus any referrals they receive from other sources. The two Barnardo's project currently work with all young women reported as missing. The Leeds project works with all young people reported missing (with the exception, currrently, of young people from residential care).[8]

Methods of contact

The main method of contact with young people for all the projects is information passed to them by the police regarding reported missing person incidents, but again there are significant differences in approach. The two Barnardo's projects receive notification from the police when a young person is reported missing, at which point they write a letter to the parents or carers introducing the project. They then receive a further notification when the young person returns home, at which point they write both to the young person and to the parent or carer. These letters are followed by a visit to the home.

At Leeds the project receives information from the police when a young person who has been reported missing returns home. The project writes both to the young person and to the parents or carers, introducing the project and proposing a date for the visit, which is then followed through unless it is cancelled by the parent or young person.

The Children's Society scheme run by Youth Link in Birmingham has piloted a variety of ways of making contact incorporating all the above methods, as discussed in more detail later in the chapter.

The ASTRA Project adopts a more direct approach, it does not send out letters to either the young person or the family, but attempts to get in touch with the young person directly, either at home, at school or by telephone.

Models of service delivery

All the projects see the initial contact with the young person as providing an opportunity for the young person to talk about any issues, and to gain information about what the project can offer them. For the two Barnardo's projects there is additionally an element of assessment in the initial contact, aimed at identifying young women who may be at risk of sexual exploitation.

Where ongoing work is provided by the projects, this is intended primarily to be short term. For example, ASTRA sees its role as being one of crisis intervention and it aims to work with young people for six to twelve weeks. Contributors stressed the need to be flexible in their response to the differing needs and circumstances of young people. A range of interventions are employed, with a focus on the issues that

8 Discussions are currently under way between Leeds City Council, The Children's Society and Save the Children (which runs the local Children's Rights Service) about the most appropriate way to provide services to this target group

led to the young person running away, and attempts are made to resolve them in order to prevent further incidents of their going missing:

> *'Our service will try and pick up a young person for an appointment or not, or meet them in the café with their mate – that would be quite normal to us, whereas some services would say, "We only visit at home" or "We only visit in school." I think that flexibility needs to be built into any role or job description that anyone creates.'*

Discussion

As the description of services has indicated, there is considerable diversity among the missing persons schemes so far set up, and there are a number of unresolved issues about the best ways to operate such schemes. These issues can be divided into two broad areas: methods of contact, and approaches to working with young people and families. There is a fair degree of inter-relationship between these two issues, and there is a need for a coherent and consistent approach to making decisions about them. There are also issues around the extent to which this kind of service is suitable for the needs of the diverse range of young people who run away. Finally, there are some common messages emanating from the projects under discussion.

Methods of contact

It is still not clear what is the most helpful method of making contact with young people (and their parents or carers) in missing persons schemes. Much may depend on the philosophy of the project and the planned nature and extent of ongoing work with young people and their carers.

An early missing persons scheme, run as a pilot by Leeds Safe House in the 1990s, used the approach of police officers circulating cards that publicised the scheme. It was hoped that young people would then make telephone contact with the project. In reality this approach did not succeed in engaging with young people. There seem to be several reasons for this. First, in practical terms, it is quite difficult for the police to ensure that cards are available for all officers and so there may well be a significant proportion of young people who do not receive any information about the scheme. A second problem is that the scheme may become associated with the police in young people's minds, and this is unlikely to facilitate their contacting the project as an independent service. In addition, it seems that young people are unlikely to make contact with such a scheme, at least in the aftermath of a running away incident, and that more active and direct approaches are needed to increase the likelihood of engaging with them.

The experience of the Birmingham scheme run by Youth Link is interesting in this respect because the project has successively piloted a number of different techniques with increasing success. The initial approach was the same as above, resulting again in very low levels of contact from young people. A second approach involved writing letters to young people inviting them to contact the service and simultaneously sending a leaflet to parents. This approach resulted in a small increase in the number of contacts. A third approach piloted was a leaflet sent to young people (including information in Widgit (a symbolic, pictorial language) aimed at young people who are not able to read) which included a postcard (postage pre-paid) that young people could return to the project requesting information, a phone call or a visit. Again there was some limited improvement in contact rates. The current approach is for the project to write to young people and parents with a proposed date for a visit, asking the young person to contact the project if they do not want the visit.

The two principal methods – the one involving letters to the young person and their parents as operated in Leeds, Birmingham, Bradford and Kirklees, and the other involving a direct attempt to contact the young person as operated in Gloucester – seem to have competing advantages. The former approach seems well received by parents, as already discussed, but the latter approach seems to more often result in an initial interview with the young person. It may also be that the initial impression created by each approach is taken as an indication of what the service can offer. The projects' strategies for making initial contact reflect different philosophies of working with young people and families, as discussed below.

The nature and goals of work

The ASTRA Project is probably the most 'young-person-centred' of the four projects under discussion in this chapter, both in terms of its method of initially contacting young people and the nature of its ongoing work with them. The project focuses strongly on the young person and carries out much of its work with them on an individual basis, although it will carry out joint work involving other members of the young person's family if this is something that the young person chooses. In the eyes of contributors, the advantage of this strong focus on young people is the ability to establish a relationship of trust with them:

> 'Young people in that situation [running away] feel they have no control, and I know that this is something that is borne out in the Still Running research and Running the Risk before that. When you feel that you have no control and the only thing you can control is where you go – what you do with your feet – the last thing you want is someone to come and try and control you again. You're not going to respond to that, so our approach, whether it's conscious or subconscious, has always started from the point of putting that young person back in control of the situation, at least trying to make them feel that that is the case.'

The other three projects, which all make initial contacts with both the young person and their carers, put more emphasis on a multi-perspective approach. They are still committed to the key principles of working with young people that are to a great extent a common feature of all the projects contributing to this report, as discussed in Chapter 8. However, they also place emphasis on gaining the acceptance of parents for their interventions:

> 'I always aim to help the young person share what they can with their parent, rather than speaking to the young person and leaving. I don't think that would help to ease tensions between parents and young people; it's not going to help them stay there next time when they have a problem.'

Without a rigorous evaluation it is impossible to draw conclusions about the pros and cons of these two different philosophies of missing persons work, but it is possible to draw on knowledge of the phenomenon of running away in order to speculate on their relative merits. The research indicates that young people who run away are often mistrustful of, or have lost their faith in, professionals and other adults. To this extent the ASTRA approach is well founded, in that it gives priority to forming a relationship with the young person. On the other hand, research also indicates that most of the reasons why young people run away are to do with problems in the home environment. Viewed from this standpoint it makes sense for projects to attempt to establish positive relationships both with young people and with key members of their family. This is clearly a matter for ongoing debate and, hopefully, evaluation, but the issue keys into broader debates about approaches to working with young people which will be picked up again in Chapter 8.

Limitations of missing persons schemes

A missing persons scheme working in isolation from a range of other services for runaways may find it difficult to engage with some young people. A particular issue is whether the project offers any emergency accommodation. Several contributors commented that the lack of an accommodation option could be a barrier to establishing an initial relationship with some young people:

> 'When they find out that I can't offer them somewhere else to be, often they lose interest in accessing other bits of the service.'

> 'Emergency accommodation is an immediate concern for [some of] the young people we work with... It's kind of half a project without that option.'

As with other models of working, a missing persons scheme may best be operated as part of a wider package of services, a point which is echoed in other parts of this report and returned to in Chapter 13.

Working with young people from minority ethnic backgrounds

There are some tentative indications that missing persons schemes may have variable success in working with the issues facing young people from minority ethnic backgrounds, although there is not yet enough practice experience to draw firm conclusions on this issue.

There are some question marks about the extent to which Asian young people are reported as missing by their families. As discussed in Chapter 10, running away may be a particularly sensitive issue for the families of young people from certain cultural backgrounds, and there is the possibility of the family being viewed negatively as a consequence. A contributor from one scheme had become aware of the potential repercussions of police arriving at a house, in uniform and in a marked car, to respond to a missing person report. The fear of drawing attention to the house may be a factor in deterring some families from reporting a missing incident to the police until it becomes absolutely necessary. Unfortunately, the ethnic origin of young people reported missing is not collected routinely by the police in missing persons reports, so it is difficult to ascertain whether there is evidence of under-reporting and there is currently insufficient data from missing persons projects to make reliable comparisons with the research findings based on self-reporting of running away by young people.

The potential of missing persons schemes to engage with young people from ethnic minority groups who are reported missing has been demonstrated, for example, by successful pieces of work at ASTRA. However, a number of contributors felt that the projects could do more to develop services in a way that is credible to families and young people in minority ethnic groups, and culturally sensitive to the contexts in which young people live.

Working with young people running away from substitute care

Some of the schemes currently do not work with young people running away from the substitute care system while others do. There is a question about the appropriateness of missing persons schemes for this group of young people, for at least two reasons. First, the reporting procedures for young people in residential care that are in operation in many local authorities mean that a large proportion of missing persons reports relate to unauthorised absences, essentially involving young people coming in later than expected. Second, many young people run away from substitute care repeatedly within relatively short periods of time, thus triggering multiple missing persons reports.

These factors suggest that there may need to be some modification to reporting and/or contacting procedures for missing persons schemes working with this target group. There is a potential role for independent professional interventions for young people running away from care, and missing persons schemes could provide a valuable safety net. They can be a means of fulfilling the recommendations of the Children's Safeguards Review that the reasons for young people going missing should be ascertained (Utting, 1997). Clearly, therefore, missing persons schemes can play an important part in a range of services for young people who run away from residential care. They might be more effective when developed in conjunction with agreed protocols regarding the reporting of young people missing from care. Such protocols are currently being put into place in many areas.

Nevertheless, they may not be the most efficient way of engaging with young people in the care system on the issue of running away. The initial attraction of missing persons schemes was the ability to make contact at an early stage with young people in the community who may not otherwise receive any professional intervention relating to the factors which led to them running away. However, in the case of young people in substitute care, bearing in mind the relatively high prevalence of running away, there is more potential for generic interventions. The Bradford Young Missing Persons Scheme has developed specific ways of working with young people in the care system (see Chapter 7).

One contributor from a missing persons scheme commented that it was particularly difficult to engage effectively with young people in substitute care who had gone missing and returned. These young people will often have had contact with a significant number of professionals throughout their lives and may perceive a visit by a worker from a missing persons scheme as an unwanted intervention. This makes it especially important to ensure that the intervention is seen by young people as being concerned with their wishes and feelings.

Relationships with parents and carers

Despite initial concerns, all the schemes report surprisingly positive reactions from parents when they make contact with them and/or young people initially as a result of a reported missing person incident:

> 'They do welcome you with open arms, which is something I've been surprised about... But we're saying that we're prepared to listen, which is something people don't [usually] get.'

Parents have often expressed relief that someone is offering some help to their child, and there has been only a small amount of gate-keeping by parents.

> 'Nearly all the parents have actually said, "I can see why my daughter needs someone to talk to who's not family, and I think it's good that it's a young person's service." A few, and a very very few, parents say, "She's getting everything, everyone comes to talk to her, no one's listening to what we want, she thinks she can get away with murder and you're helping her to do that." It's very, very rare. I think that parents see that young people do need an adult and they put quite a lot of trust in what you are going to say in response. Having a social work background, I would have thought that parents thought that having another professional turning up on their door, they're going to be asking loads of questions about "have I abused them" – that type of conversation – but it hasn't been like that. Parents have willingly gone out of the room and sat in the kitchen for an hour while we've had a chat.'

The success of the projects in this respect is encouraging. However, it must be borne in mind that many incidents of running away are not reported to the police. It seems likely that, on the whole, the projects are coming into contact with those parents who are most concerned about their child's welfare and, therefore, are most likely to welcome intervention.

One of the difficulties that projects have encountered in ongoing work relates to parents' own need for support. In many cases, the parents are struggling with issues of their own, and it is clear that they are not receiving support from other agencies. The projects have had to clarify with parents that their role is to focus on the young person. However, workers have often experienced frustration that the needs of the family are not being met, and have ended up feeling that if these issues could be resolved then the young person's problems would be diminished.

Independence

One of the areas of consensus among the projects contributing to the study is about the need for missing persons schemes to be seen as independent from statutory services in order to engage effectively with young people and parents. Young people who run away may have already had contact with statutory services (although research suggests that this is not the case for the majority of first-time missing incidents) or they may have preconceptions or fears about the intervention of the police or social services in their lives:

> 'Young people see the word "police", or an association with the police, and they switch off. But if you have that face-to-face contact... they're usually prepared to hear you out.'

These fears may also be felt by parents and carers, who again may also have had previous involvement with these services:

> '*They think that it's good that we're not social services, it's very good that we are a charity and it's good that we've had an immediate response, and they appear to be very willing to want help and want someone to listen to what they've got to say.*'

There is a paradox here, in that, among the projects contributing to this publication, it is the ones running missing persons schemes which have the closest links with both statutory and voluntary agencies in their area, as discussed below. Indeed, the ASTRA project is technically a statutory service, as it receives core funding from statutory sources (social services, education and the police).

So, it is the *perceived* independence of projects which is important. This independence needs to be balanced with the need to have good links with other agencies in order to be able to facilitate young people's access to the range of services that can meet their diverse needs.

Speed of response

A second area of consensus concerns the value of a speedy response to running away. One of the reasons that the projects seem to have been particularly welcomed by young people and adults alike is that they are often able to make a visit within a day or two of the young person's return home. Again, this is sometimes experienced as a contrast to previous involvement with voluntary and statutory services:

> '*A lot of young people and parents have commented that we've turned up very quickly because a lot of the responses from other professionals have been lengthy waiting lists and lengthy response, and at the end of the wait they've been told that there's going to be no services.*'

It seems that this may be a particularly important aspect that should be consciously built in to a missing persons scheme in terms of resourcing, in order that the scheme can take advantage of the goodwill it engenders.

Multi-agency involvement in the schemes

The issue of partnership with other agencies is covered in detail in Chapter 9. However, the value of multi-agency involvement at an advisory or managerial level has been particularly emphasised by contributors from the missing persons schemes, and this seems worthy of brief mention in this chapter, particularly as the viability of these schemes is almost completely dependent on the co-operation of the police.

The Gloucester and Kirklees projects both originated in statutory services initiatives, and the Bradford project emanated from the multi-agency steering group of an existing Barnardo's project. In the case of ASTRA, one contributor saw the multi-agency involvement in the scheme, right from its inception, as the key factor in its success:

> '*The major strength of the project is the steering group... they've been involved from the beginning, they conceived the idea collectively and have been supportive of it since. It's an amalgamation of voluntary and statutory sector organisations, all of whom have found a common interest in supporting this initiative and have stuck with it when they could have lost interest or found other initiatives that*

were more kind of flavour of the month, really. That's the key strength and I fundamentally believe that we wouldn't have reached the point we've reached so far without that kind of inter-agency support and co-operation. And it's something that we've become aware is quite unique. Across the rest of the country, there are other projects doing similar work and they are largely voluntary sector projects, and they often have difficulty getting senior level support from statutory services.'

It is notable also that in all three of these areas, there was a recognition of the need for such a scheme because of the emergence of issues at a local level (the West case in Gloucester, and evidence of links between running away and the sexual exploitation of young people in the other two projects).

It seems particularly advisable, therefore, to place emphasis on gaining the support and commitment of local agencies, in particular police and social services, from the inception of these schemes. If possible, this should include building the scheme on the foundations of locally identified concerns or locally initiated research.

Key points

- Appropriate methods of contact are key to the success of missing persons schemes. Passive models which rely on young people taking the initiative have proved unsuccessful, and there is a need to be more active, through letters and through visiting young people and/or their families.

- Parents and carers have generally responded positively to the interventions of missing persons schemes, viewing them as a service which can help the young person. There has been surprisingly little hostility towards workers.

- However, since not all young runaways are reported as missing to the police, projects relying solely on police referrals will, by definition, only reach a proportion of all young runaways, and therefore do not constitute a universal intervention.

- In developing a missing persons scheme, a fairly fundamental decision needs to be made about the extent to which the scheme focuses on the young person, or on the whole family. This will have implications both for the initial reception of the scheme's intervention and also for its ability to carry out ongoing work to prevent further running away incidents.

- Missing persons schemes may need to develop a slightly different model of working with young people in residential care, given the high volume of reported missing incidents, many of which are essentially 'unauthorised absences' rather than incidents of 'running away'. Nevertheless, they can play an important role as a safety net.

- The perceived independence of missing persons schemes from social services and the police is believed by contributors to be an important ingredient in their ability to engage with young people and families.

- Initiating a rapid response when the young person returns home is also regarded as important.

- Missing persons schemes may not be as effective at engaging with young people from minority ethnic backgrounds, as it seems that these young people may well be less likely to be reported as missing when they run away.

- Good inter-agency working seems particularly important for an effective missing persons scheme, and evidently the support of the police is an essential requirement.

6

CENTRE-BASED SERVICES

Introduction

This chapter looks at two projects which work with young people who run away as part of a wider range of services offered to young people focused around a drop-in/advice centre: the Home & Away Project in Lambeth run by the Catholic Children's Society, and Checkpoint in Torquay run by The Children's Society. These projects both aim to undertake short-term work with young people and their families, with a principal aim of re-establishing young people within their family or community where possible. Both projects also aim to provide very short-term emergency accommodation for young people in certain circumstances.

Case studies

CASE STUDY 1

Home & Away Project, London   *Catholic Children's Society*

The idea for the Home & Away Project originated in a piece of research undertaken by the Catholic church in central London. It found that many young homeless people sleeping on the streets of the central city area came from Lambeth in south London. The project was therefore set up to cater for the needs of these young people within their local area. It is managed by the Catholic Children's Society and currently receives much of its funding from Lambeth Social Services.

The project works with young people aged 13 to 20. Its main aims are to prevent young people becoming homeless and to prevent young people being accommodated by the local authority. So a focus of its work is to try to resolve the family situations that threaten to make young people homeless.

One aspect of the project's work is a crisis team which works with young people under the age of 18. This team uses a solution-focused brief therapy approach to work with young people and their families. It is also able to provide emergency accommodation to some of the young people with whom it works, including some emergency foster care provision, which is accessible to young people under the age of 16, with parental consent.

CASE STUDY 2

Checkpoint, Torquay   *The Children's Society*

Checkpoint has been working with young people in Torbay since the early 1990s. In 1998 it became a project in its own right. It provides a range of services for young people, using a 'hub and spoke' model. The 'hub' of the service is a general drop-in centre for young people, staffed primarily by volunteers. This centre has over 6,000 contacts per year with young people. The 'spokes' of the model are a collection of specialist services, including a counselling service, a service focusing on sexual health, and so on. In 1999, using Children's Promise funding, a specific runaways service – the South Coast Runaways Initiative (SCRI) – was added to the project to work with under-18s.

The SCRI is a service offered to appropriate young people coming into the Checkpoint drop-in centre. Young people are referred to the specialist runaways worker who will undertake short-term focused work with the young person. Linked to this work, the project is developing a model of emergency accommodation for young people for up to four nights. The SCRI has also recently begun a pilot scheme providing independent interviews for young people who run away from residential care in Torbay.

Description of work

Target groups

Both projects aim to work with young people who run away and with those at imminent risk of running away or being forced to leave home. The minimum age for both projects is set at 13 years. The emphasis of both projects appears to be on young people who are still relatively attached to their families.

Methods of contact with young people

For both projects the primary source of work with young people who run away is through a drop-in centre. Home & Away also receives initial contacts from young people over the telephone, but this is usually followed up by a meeting at the centre. Word-of-mouth recommendation is an important source of referrals for both projects, although in both cases some outreach work into schools has also been undertaken.

Models of service delivery

The Home & Away Project has an explicit theoretical framework for engaging with young people and their families: solution-focused brief therapy. As its name implies, this approach is concerned not with problems but with solutions:

> *'Solution-focused brief therapy isn't concerned with problems, it's about solutions and how to help people to draw on their own strengths and what already works. Because in most crises people can identify something that has worked before or something positive... People can come up with their own solutions and we can support them through that... It sounds really mad but it works – I was really cynical about it when I started.'*

One of the potential advantages of this approach is that young people and parents will sometimes already have had experience of other agencies which focused on the problems they were facing, and will have found these to be unhelpful. The project can therefore bring a fresh, positive approach to the issues; this often provides a positive experience for families and distinguishes the project's work from that of statutory agencies. Solution-focused therapy is intended to last only a short time and the project rarely works with young people and families for more than 12 weeks. If there are issues that are more engrained, the project will refer the case on to other agencies.

The Home & Away Project has two emergency foster carers who can accommodate young people for up to 72 hours. The carers are approved by the Catholic Children's Society and by Lambeth Social Services. They are paid a retainer, plus a nightly fee when they provide accommodation. This service is mainly intended as a respite for young people and their families while the project is working with them on solutions to the situation. Mostly it is used for young people who are at risk of leaving home. Accommodation for under-16s is always provided with parental consent, although this has rarely been an issue. In certain circumstances young people who have already had to leave home can be accommodated with the emergency foster carers, again with parental consent.

The SCRI uses a young-person-centred approach which recognises the diversity of situations of young people who run away. Thus it can provide a range of services:

> 'The service young people get very much depends on what they want. Some people just want information and advice. Some people want to break the ice with their parents, so they want crisis mediation work. Some people want more in-depth work.'

There is an initial assessment interview in which the worker explores with the young person the reasons for their situation and what they would like to do about it. The model is broadly a crisis intervention framework:

> 'My initial assessment will be exploring with them why they are in the situation they're in and what they want to do about that, and looking at where we take it from there. It's crisis intervention, so on average I guess I'm in their lives about four days... The most I've engaged with someone has been six weeks, and that was because other services weren't kicking into place.'

The worker is able to refer young people to other parts of the Checkpoint service for specialist counselling and other assistance.

The project has also been developing a model of flexible refuge provision. The idea of this is to provide temporary supported accommodation for young people on an occasional basis for no more than four nights, at selected bed-and-breakfast establishments. The establishments will have been prepared for the possibility of this kind of work. The project aims to employ sessional workers to support the young people during these periods, two workers working at once. In the daytime the young person will then use the Checkpoint facilities and the SCRI specialist worker to attempt to find a longer-term solution to their situation. This project has been endorsed by the local police and has the support of the local Social Services Department. However, some legal issues have arisen in relation to Section 51 of the Children Act, and the current plan is to provide this accommodation only where parental consent can be gained.

Discussion

Self-referral

A key aspect of both centre-based services is that the onus of accessing the service lies primarily with the young person. This is in contrast to the missing persons schemes discussed in the previous chapter, which actively seek out young people who have run away and returned home.

This aspect can be viewed as both a strength and a weakness of these services. On the downside, research has shown that many young people who run away are not aware of the helping services that are available in their area. A centre-based service relying on self-referral is therefore likely to meet only a portion of the total need in the local area, unless it has a very well-developed profile among young people under the age of 16. Even where awareness is high, there is the potential barrier of young people having to take the plunge and enter the centre, rather than be met initially on their own territory.

On the other hand, the young people who do access these services are likely to be motivated to find solutions to their problems. Both projects report high levels of success, either in terms of being able to negotiate a return home with a resolution to the some of the problems that caused young people to run away or contemplate running away, or in terms of finding young people other places to stay within the community. Of 48 young people worked with by the SCRI in its first year of operation, 19 returned home, 14 moved to other accommodation in the community (extended family, friends, etc.) and, of the remainder, only three chose to remain on the streets. These were young people who had already been away from home for several months when they made contact with the project.

Reaching young people not in contact with other services

Both projects aim to work with young people who are not in contact with other services and have been successful in achieving this aim. The SCRI was set up with the aim of targeting a specific group of young people:

> *'One of the aims when we set this up was to capture young people who weren't accessing help from any other service, and that's what we've done. The majority of young people we work with, at the time they engage with us, are receiving no other help from anywhere else. That's where we saw the gap.'*

The Home & Away Project will not do substantial pieces of work with young people who have a social worker or who are involved with the youth offending team, although it will undertake short-term telephone advocacy with these young people to ensure that other agencies are meeting their needs.

In reality, then, despite the concerns mentioned above about publicity and awareness-raising, the experience of the two projects illustrates the potential for a centre-based model to engage with young people who are not already receiving support in connection with the problems they are experiencing.

Integration of services for young people

One of the strengths of both projects is that the services they offer young people who run away are part of a wider integrated network of services that they provide. This has several advantages. First, the service may be seen by young people to be less stigmatising than a service known to work exclusively with young people who run away. This certainly seems to be the case at Checkpoint where young people with specific problems can remain fairly anonymous among the thousands of young people contacting the centre for a variety of reasons:

> 'What it means for young people is that you're not immediately identified as somebody who has a drug and alcohol problem or somebody who has run away, because you're just turning up with lots of other young people... So young people are relatively anonymous and are not singled out or stigmatised.'

Second, there is the possibility of young people gaining access to an integrated range of services. At Home & Away this includes the possibility of young people under 18 being supported beyond their 18th birthday in independent housing accessed through the project. In the case of Checkpoint there is the possibility of access to other specialist services focusing on relevant issues, such as sexual health, within the same project.

At project level, a further advantage of an integrated centre-based model is the economies of scale it offers. At Checkpoint, the SCRI consists primarily of one specialist project worker. However, this initiative enjoys the benefits of being part of a larger concern in terms of front-line drop-in centre access, telephone support, and so on.

The need for emergency accommodation

It is interesting that both projects include an emergency accommodation element. As noted in Chapter 3, one of the concerns about a model which has refuge provision as its central component is that young people may feel that they have no option but to move into a refuge in order to access the project's other services, such as advocacy, counselling or mediation. It seems that the centre-based models are able to work with the majority of young people without providing accommodation. Often, where young people have run away, it is possible to find a place to stay for a few nights with extended family or friends. However, in a minority of cases this is not possible, and it is in these cases that emergency accommodation is or would be provided:

> 'The criteria for the refuge is that they are going to be at serious significant risk if they don't access the refuge. One example of that is a young woman aged 15, returned to a squat where [there were] six older men involved with various different drug uses and offending. She would have fitted the criteria [but most young people] generally have support elsewhere, either with extended family or with friends.'

The case of the SCRI is particularly interesting in this respect because, for the first year of its existence, the project has not been able to offer an accommodation option. This has provided the unexpected opportunity for an assessment of what the need for accommodation might be. The SCRI specialist worker undertook a review of the 48 cases worked with in the first 12 months of the service, and estimated that 13 or 14 of these young people would have fitted the envisaged criteria for flexible refuge, i.e., that they would be at serious risk if they did not get access to refuge. An example of this was the young woman in the above quote who was staying at a squat with older men involved with drugs and offending, and who had no other emergency accommodation options. So the project estimates that around one-quarter of the young people it works with might need flexible refuge when it becomes available. This is much the same as the proportion of young people who report sleeping rough when they run away (Safe on the Streets Research Team, 1999). Similarly, the Home & Away Project provides emergency foster care accommodation, mostly on a respite basis, for an estimated 20 young people per year.

These projects provide evidence, then, of a need among a significant minority of young people who run away for some emergency accommodation. However, there is a suggestion that access to this service should be controlled. As one contributor noted, most of the young people running away who approach the centre present themselves as having accommodation needs, even though they have somewhere temporary to stay:

> 'They probably come in saying... Presenting it as an accommodation need, actually, and that's because often, as you know, what happens is that young people don't make a planned move to run away. It'll often be a culmination of events, as something will happen – which might appear quite minor to other people – that will trigger it and they will think, "That's it." So it's un-thought-out and therefore there's no plan as to what they're going to do. So when they come in to see me often what I'm trying to do is to slow the process down for them and actually give them the opportunity to think about what are they going to do now. So, whereas they'll often come in here and say, "I'm 15 and I'm not going back home, I've got nowhere to live", so they present it as they've got nowhere to live. When you actually break it down for them and explore what the different things are, then they're able to come up with, "Actually, I could stay with Gran" or "I could stay with a friend for a couple of days", or whatever it takes, really, while you sort things out. But there are some that you just know, if you had the refuge, that things would just work so much better.'

Relationships with parents

The centre-based projects work in a way that often entails involvement with the families of the young people who run away. As with the missing persons schemes, the general experience of contributors was that their intervention was welcomed by parents and carers:

> 'When I started this work, that's where I thought the problem would be... very angry parents. And that's been the biggest shock, in that none have expressed any kind of negative feelings about the work that's being done. In the main, what they've said is, "Thank God that there's somewhere for my son or daughter to go", and I think it's about how you present it... What I'll always try to do is to explain what my role is – to find a solution to the problem and also to encourage young people to reestablish themselves in the community somewhere, somewhere that's safe. And I think once you explain that to parents, they're OK.'

Both projects reported that parents were often glad that someone was trying to help, and also that many of the families with whom they have contact have already sought help from other agencies with limited success:

> 'By the time a young person presents to me, things are quite dire, and the chances are, in the main, that parents have been trying to get help, or young people have

been trying to get help from different quarters over a period of months, sometimes years, and feeling that they've been passed around.'

There also do not appear to be any major difficulties in gaining parental consent for young people to be accommodated temporarily elsewhere. The Home & Away Project has had hardly any difficulties over this, although it mainly uses its emergency foster carers for respite:

'We try to keep that resource available for the young people where we are working together with the family anyway, so we would be talking to the families about it and offering it as an option.'

At Checkpoint, despite concerns before the project started working with young people, the specialist worker does not now foresee any major problems with seeking parental consent for flexible refuge.

The need for long-term referral options

While a short-term intervention can be effective in resolving immediate issues for many young people who run away, research indicates that there are often longer-term underlying contextual factors contributing to the pattern of running away. In some cases these factors will require a much more substantial intervention, and contributors at both projects mentioned the need to refer some young people and families on to specialist, longer-term family services:

'Particularly working with runaways under the age of 16, getting a response from social services, that's a major issue. There's always the problem of young people engaging with us and we can take things so far but after that, where do we go? We have one worker, we can't provide that longer-term support. We can do the patching things up, looking for opportunities, helping young people take them, and working with families initially, but only for a very short time – then where do we go? And that may be a problem for other projects in other local authority areas where they don't have good family support services.'

A project offering short-term centre-based intervention therefore will need to develop good links with other specialist services in the locality. However, this can be difficult for young people:

'My work is very crisis-led. I'm not in their lives for very long and one of the young people did actually say that that for her was a difficulty because it was the first time that somebody had actually listened to her, and that what I would have to do is pass her on to other parts of the service. So I think the advantage is that everything is on site here. The disadvantage is that specialist workers do their specific piece of work and then it goes over to somebody else, and if you can forge a relationship with somebody, for that young person that's quite difficult.'

Where such services are not available, there is a danger that the model of working described in this chapter will face the same problem of repetitive usage by some young people that was the drawback of the short-term crisis intervention model operated in refuges, as discussed in Chapter 3.

Key points

- Centre-based services, being partly reliant on self-referral by young people, need to pay particular attention to publicity and awareness-raising, as there is evidence that young people who run away are not always aware of services available to them in their locality.

- However, both projects considered in this chapter have been successful in engaging with young people who are not already in contact with other helping agencies.

- Situating services for runaways within a centre providing a range of services for young people offers the possibility of an integrated approach to work which can meet a diverse range of needs both in the short and the longer term.

- There is a need, among a significant minority of young people using centre-based projects, for short-term emergency accommodation, and it may be that such projects are best located as one component within a network of services for young people who run away.

- In common with the missing persons schemes discussed in Chapter 5, the projects in this chapter have undertaken a considerable amount of work with families and report a positive reception to their work from parents and carers.

- The short-term interventions of the centre-based projects can be effective in resolving immediate issues, but some young people and their families will require a more substantial longer-term intervention and, therefore, projects adopting this model will need either to cater for these needs or to establish good links with other specialist services in the locality, such as family therapy services.

7

OTHER PRACTICE MODELS

The models explored in the previous four chapters have been the main methods utilised to date in the UK for working with young people who run away. However, some other methods have been employed, although most of these are currently at an early stage of development. This chapter looks briefly at these alternative models and summarises some of the early learning from practice.

Schools-based preventive work

Schools are a common location for preventive strategies aimed at social issues affecting young people. Schools-based interventions were a key suggestion made by young runaways who were asked what kind of help might have prevented them having to run away (Safe on the Streets Research Team, 1999).

CASE STUDY 1

Peer Counselling Scheme, Leeds *The Children's Society*

Safe on the Streets – Leeds has developed a model of peer counselling in schools in an attempt to provide early interventions for young people who may be at risk of running away. Project staff deliver a training programme to young people who are interested in becoming peer counsellors (usually in the 15- to 17-year-old age group), covering basic counselling skills. These young people then become available as a resource within the school for young people who are having problems either at home, at school or in their personal lives. This kind of model is quite common in North America as a way of tackling a range of issues, including running away.

The above scheme has been implemented in five secondary schools in Leeds over the past three years. The training programme has been successful in recruiting and preparing pupils to be peer counsellors, and young people's enthusiasm for, and commitment to, this work has been high.

The take-up of the counselling service has varied significantly across schools and at different times. From the experience so far, it appears that the culture of the school and the commitment of its staff are important factors affecting the scheme's success in a given school. The scheme has worked best when there has been a dedicated member of staff who liaises with the project worker and supports young people:

> '*What we have found is that you need some strong allies in the school... You need to get not just one teacher on board, but a number of committed individuals,*

to include at least one person who will drive it in the school. Particularly as an outside agency going in, it's quite hard. I think one way we might change or develop it in the future is to establish a stronger base in the school.'

There have been issues around the provision of confidential space for counselling to take place within the school, and this also seems to have a significant bearing on levels of usage. It has sometimes been difficult to identify a suitable location in which counselling can take place which is both private and accessible. A variety of techniques have been tried to facilitate young people's access to the scheme: for example, offering a drop-in lunchtime facility, or having a postbox through which young people can make contact with the peer counsellors. There is a need to tailor the methods of contact to the contexts in individual schools.

Given the nature of the peer counselling work, it is important to have a clear awareness of child protection issues, to include these in the training of peer counsellors, and to have agreements with the schools about how to handle any issues which do arise. Although child protection issues have not been a common feature of the work in practice, some issues of emotional and physical abuse have emerged through the counselling and these have been referred on to a designated specialist teacher in the school.

A key issue has been that of focusing the scheme on the intended target audience. This is a problem common to all preventive projects. It is not easy to identify young people at risk of running away, and so there is a risk of the scheme becoming a generic counselling scheme. To an extent this appears to have happened at times, with school bullying being a common issue brought to counselling. The project is considering accompanying the scheme with awareness-raising in the school about the issue of running away in order to focus use of the service more effectively.

However, this issue can be perceived by schools as a sensitive or a minority issue, and this has necessitated the project taking a broad approach to the scheme's goals in order for it to be regarded as acceptable and relevant by schools:

'Even if it's recognised as something that is worthwhile in itself, they don't see it as something with a broad appeal or substantial base of need within their environment. So we've adopted a broad approach to get over people's barriers about how many young people it would be appropriate for.'

The project is currently considering whether it is possible to develop a model of peer support which can work in primary schools, bearing in mind the research findings about the early onset of running away among young people who run away repeatedly, as reviewed in Chapter 2.

Internet work

Youth Link in Birmingham has recently developed a website and e-mail service around the issue of young people running away. One of the initial motivations for this was to offer a service to disabled young people:

'It started as a way of offering something to young people with disabilities. Physically disabled young people can't literally run away but they can run away in their heads.'

However, it was also seen as having a potentially wider value as one of a range of preventive strategies to assist young people at risk of running away:

> 'It's another way for young people to get in touch with us, to find someone who can help them, before they run away.'

The website provides information about issues including running away, safe sex and drugs. It also informs young people about their rights, and about potential other sources of help for young people (including a links page).

Young people can write to the project via e-mail to seek support or further information, and will receive a response from a project worker within 24 working hours. The project has some concerns about becoming involved in an ongoing personal e-mail relationship with young people. In order to minimise the chance of this developing, workers respond to e-mails on a rota basis and young people who e-mail are encouraged to telephone or visit the project or to seek help from other suggested resources.

The service is still in the early stages of development, but there have already been a number of e-mail contacts from young people who are facing difficulties that might lead to them running away. So far there have been very few problems relating to inappropriate use of the e-mail service. This development therefore provides some indication of the potential for this kind of initiative to be part of a preventive approach to the issue of running away.

Family-based work

Given the strong link between family issues and running away, it is surprising that so little attention has been paid to developing services specifically to work with families in order to resolve the issues that lead to young people running away.

A small pilot project was recently set up by NCH and attached to the London refuge. The aim was to work with families of young people using the refuge in order to prevent repeat incidence of running away. This pilot has now finished and the project has moved on to other areas of work. Unfortunately, it was not possible to gain views from the project to contribute to this report.

Some of the projects described earlier in the report have focused on family work, the prime example being the solution-focused therapy undertaken by the Home & Away Project (Chapter 6). It is interesting to note that this approach has also been used by The Children's Society's SANDS Project – a family intervention project which developed out of the closure of the Southside Refuge in Bournemouth.

Safe on the Streets – Leeds intends to develop a new scheme working with families of young people who run away, using the family group conferencing model. The whole area of family work in relation to young people running away is a potentially fertile one for development, both in a general sense and also in order to meet effectively the needs of young people and families from some minority ethnic groups, as discussed in Chapter 10.

Work with young people in care

Given the high rates of running away among young people in substitute care, this is an obvious sub-group on which to target specific interventions. Several contributing projects have developed or are in the process of developing specific work with young people in substitute care, particularly those in children's homes.

Safe in the City has developed a model of preventive group work with young people in residential units in Manchester. This idea stemmed from an awareness of the high proportion of young people on the streets in the city centre who were running away from care settings. It was felt that these young people might best be worked with when they were not in this situation but in a period of relative stability. The project therefore approached the local Social Services Department (SSD) with a proposal to run group-work sessions for young people in residential units to discuss the issue of running away and, possibly, to play a preventive role in terms of repeat incidence. This proposal was taken up by the SSD and the terms of engagement with young people were negotiated.

Significantly, it was agreed that the project workers could adhere to the project's confidentiality policy when working with young people in the units. It was found that in addition to having a tight confidentiality policy, it was also particularly important in residential settings to be seen to be adhering to the policy:

> 'It's difficult in units because they are public places. I think making people feel safe is about how you enact confidentiality and how you behave, really. An example would be that we would make sure we didn't talk to [residential] staff after the group, even just to say, "Hi, how are you?" We would be really cautious not to be seen to have contact with staff because young people might suspect that we were sharing information even though we said we wouldn't... You've got to be sensitive to the dynamics.'

The work consisted of a six- to eight-week course of group-work sessions. The aims of the work were to provide advice, information and education for young people when they were in a more stable setting and also to build up good relationships with residential staff. The scheme was positively received by young people. As a result of the work, the project received telephone calls from young people, which offered the opportunity to prevent further running away incidents:

> 'One of the outcomes was that young people made contact with the project for advice and information when there was something troubling them. They felt better able to do that, having been part of that group work process. So we got calls from young people and there was a lot of ability to interact with somebody before anything became problematic for them.'

Another outcome of the work was that discussion from group sessions spilled over into dialogue between young people and key workers in units. Although initially some staff in the units had concerns about the scheme, they ultimately viewed it positively. There was good feedback from the SSD and the project was subsequently asked to do similar work in other residential units.

The Bradford Young Missing Persons Scheme has also established a good working relationship with residential units and has developed tailor-made approaches for working with young people in the care system with a focus on preventing running away and sexual exploitation. This has included a mobile library of books, videos and other resources which are made available to young people in the unit to raise awareness of the risks they would be facing.

Other developments with young people in care are in the pipeline. Checkpoint in Torquay and the two Barnardo's missing persons projects in West Yorkshire have all been involved in the development of local protocols with statutory services in relation to young people running away from residential care. The Bradford and Torquay projects are about to start providing independent interviews to young people who run away from residential care on their return to the unit.

Work with young people at risk of sexual exploitation

Research suggests a strong link between young people running away and young people being sexually exploited. The Streets and Lanes Project in Bradford run by Barnardo's was set up to work specifically with young women being sexually exploited. It developed an understanding of the 'grooming' process though which young women were recruited into prostitution, and it was evident that this process often took place while a young woman had run away from her usual address (family or substitute care). Thus the primary motivation for the missing persons scheme described in Chapter 5 which emerged from that project was to attempt to identify young women at risk of sexual exploitation and to undertake preventive work. A similar principle underpinned the development of the Kirklees missing persons scheme, also discussed in Chapter 5.

The NSPCC has developed a specific project aimed at the issue of young women being sexually exploited in London: the Breaking Free Project.

CASE STUDY 2

Breaking Free Project, London   *NSPCC*

The Breaking Free Project was set up in 1999 as a result of growing awareness of young people being sexually exploited and of the lack of services to meet their needs. Much of this awareness came out of the (then) Centrepoint/NSPCC Refuge in London. Workers at the project found it difficult to undertake work with these young people because of their complex, long-term needs.

The project has developed two aspects to its direct work with young people. First, it provides a weekly drop-in session at an established centre for young people who are homeless in central London. Second, it accepts referrals from local authorities in London and other agencies to undertake individual work with young women who are being, or are thought to be at risk of being, sexually exploited. The project also offers training and consultancy with professionals in other agencies.

One of the ideas behind the project was to attempt to prevent young people becoming entrenched in a street lifestyle involving survival sex:

> *'The police... were regularly making contact with vulnerable young people and were concerned at the lack of appropriate services. In their experience, if a child or young person was new to the West End they were likely to be much easier to*

*engage and work with. If, however, they continued to spend time in the area,
they became entrenched in a street lifestyle, and working with them became very
difficult... After a period of six weeks on the streets a positive outcome for a young
person was far less likely.' (Breaking Free Project – Initial Project Report,
NSPCC, 2000)*

Looking firstly at the work of the project outside the West End, some of the young
women being referred to the project fitted the Barnardo's 'grooming' model.
They were generally young women who had already become detached from their
families, and usually would also have had some involvement with social services,
including periods of living in the substitute care system. Many of these young
women were highly mobile, and one of the strengths of the project was its ability to
remain in contact with the young people while they moved from one local authority
area to another, providing some continuity of support in what were often fairly
chaotic lives.

In terms of the work with young people in the West End, there was much less
evidence of entry into sexual exploitation through the 'grooming' model, and more
likelihood of the need for survival being a key element in young people's
involvement. The issues faced by the project in their city-centre work are very similar
to those described in Chapter 4 on street-work services. Many of the young people
are extremely detached from mainstream society and mistrustful of adults:

*'I think for the young people in the West End the issues are very different, they
are at a chaotic stage and the work you do with them is very different. You
might spend an awful lot of time engaging with them and establishing a
relationship.'*

Therefore the project has twin goals of harm minimisation together with the
long-term possibility of sometimes being able to facilitate young people moving off
the streets:

*'Harm minimisation is, I think, where you have to start with young people,
especially when they've got to where they've got to – they're not wanting to be
rescued, they are often very "anti" all services. They often just want to be left
alone and so you need to start from where they're at. They're at the stage where
they are on the streets using drugs and selling sex, and so you say, "OK, then
what can we do to make that life safer for you?"'*

The process of engaging with young people in these contexts can be very protracted
and the project has become aware of the need to set realistic goals on an individual
basis:

*'There's one young woman... for two years we've been out and she's been around,
and it's been almost impossible to make contact with her. Success now is that
when we do do outreach work and she sees us, she doesn't run off – I can offer to
buy her a drink or something and say "Hi!" and she'll know we're not the police.
Now that's a breakthrough and it's taken almost two years.'*

In other cases the project has been successful in engaging at an early stage to prevent
young people becoming entrenched, as envisaged in the conception of the project.
The project has a specific child protection orientation (both the current workers

have statutory social work experience) and this has been recognised by other agencies as one of the strengths of the service:

> *'It's often how you present the concern, semantics even sometimes, and the street-work agencies I work with, very youth-work-oriented, and they are often really exasperated with the responses they get and end up in a real head-to-head. It's been pointed out to me by some of those agencies that they've noticed the difference – if I'm in a meeting I'll try to elicit collaboration and working together in a different way.'*

One of the difficulties of using a drop-in-based model with this target group is that young people may not be wish or be able to attend at pre-arranged times. The project therefore has undertaken some outreach work and has also developed strong links with other agencies providing outreach in the West End. In general, the contributors from the project emphasised the need for good multi-agency working with this target group, a point which is discussed in more depth in Chapter 9.

Key points

- Preventive strategies in relation to running away have really only just begun to be developed in the UK. Schemes have been piloted in schools and via the Internet. At this stage it is too early to say how effective these strategies might be, and there is a need for evaluation of these initiatives and for more consideration to be given to the development of other preventive models.

- There has been relatively little family-focused work done specifically with young runaways in the UK. This is surprising, given the central importance of family relationships as a factor influencing running away (see Chapter 2). This is a key area for development in this field.

- There are very high rates of running away from residential care and there is scope for targeted initiatives aimed at this group of young people. One example is presented in this chapter which shows the potential for engaging with young people and staff in residential units to prevent repeat running away and to ensure that young people who do run away have access to services.

- There is also a strong link between sexual exploitation and running away, and several initiatives have been developed to work specifically with young people who are being, or who are at risk of being, sexually exploited on the streets. These projects can have positive outcomes in terms of harm minimisation, preventing entrenchment on the streets, providing a continuity of contact with young people with chaotic and mobile lifestyles, and facilitating co-ordination with other services to meet their needs.

8

APPROACHES TO WORKING WITH YOUNG PEOPLE

This chapter looks at the approaches projects take in engaging with young people and carrying out work with them. There is, of course, some diversity in approaches between projects. However, there is also a large amount of common ground. To a great extent all the projects that contributed to this report share a common philosophy in terms of the way they view young people and work with them. This philosophy is often referred to as a 'young-person-centred' approach. The first part of this chapter is spent exploring the key elements of this approach and some of its implications. The remainder of the chapter covers some of the more concrete elements of practice, including ways of engaging initially with young people, advocacy work, confidentiality and child protection issues, as well as some different approaches used by specific contributing projects.

Young-person-centred approach

> 'We try and take an approach with young people that it's their choice to be in touch with us, so that everything has to stem from that. Everything we do has to stem from it being their choice, so you can talk through all the options and then they have to choose whichever option they want – with support, obviously – and whilst we may feel that the option they have chosen was completely and utterly wrong, unless it was an unsafe choice we let them run with that, on the clear understanding that if or when it all goes horribly wrong, they can come back to us.'

The young-person-centred approach used by the projects is characterised by a number of key elements. These include:
- an emphasis on listening to young people
- taking seriously what young people say, and using their views and concerns as a starting point for planning the work
- providing them with information about their options and then supporting them to make informed choices
- not telling young people what to do
- working at the young person's pace
- keeping young people involved and/or informed about progress
- being non-judgemental
- not seeking parental consent
- giving young people as much control as possible over the information held about them. (See discussion about confidentiality later in this chapter.)

The list on page 62 is compiled from comments by various contributors. It was sometimes difficult to get contributors to explain this approach fully, and the reason for this seems to have been that it was almost taken for granted as the right way of working with this group of young people – one contributor described it as 'bog standard' youth work practice. It is clearly not an approach unique to working with young people who run away. However, using it with this target group of young people raises a number of issues which will be explored in the course of this chapter. Several contributors described the approach as 'treating young people like adults' and it seems that to a great extent this is what the projects aim to do. But there are clearly a number of complexities inherent in working with young people who run away that belie this simple way of describing the work, as will become clear.

Before going on to discuss some of the specific issues raised by the approach, it is important to note that some contributors expressed concern about the way the notion of a young-person-centred approach could be interpreted in practice.

One issue raised was that the approach could lead to a tendency to inertia in some cases. Adhering to the approach could leave workers feeling that they could not take any initiative, and that everything had to be instigated by young people:

> 'Young-person-centred sometimes meant for individual workers that we weren't getting off our backsides and doing things sometimes which were necessary for that young person to move their circumstances on and give them some new opportunities. We felt that too often young-person-centred might mean, "Well, I have to wait for it to come from the young person before I can act", and that became a reactive process.'

On the other hand there is a risk when working with this target group of placing too much pressure on young people, which can set them up to fail:

> 'I'm very aware that young people can feel that they've let workers down, or their family down. Their low self-esteem often means that they feel they're no good, so we try very hard to encourage them to make different choices... But also to say if they aren't able to, then we'll still be here.'

A second related concern was the distinction between being young-person-focused and young-person-led:

> '[There was a confusion over] being young-person-centred and when that became young-person-led, and that we always had to take what the young person was saying at face value and not to question that... that has not always been the case, but it is one of the things that I think we have grappled with.'

Third, as voiced in the quote above, there are some concerns about the concept of always believing what young people say:

> 'If a young person or child came expressing certain allegations, views, his or her story, what the project did was, prima facie it would accept that view up to the time when substantial evidence to the contrary came into the picture. That meant that one was required to believe what children and young people said to you, until such time as something concrete came in from the outside to contradict it... Whether that's good or bad I'm not commenting on, but how some workers

dealt with that was to line themselves up uncritically behind young people, and that's as dangerous as lining yourself up uncritically with anyone else. There was an idea that there was a moral purity about young people, and the reverse for the rest of the system – that young people were inherently good.'

In reality, however, the approach that has developed in most projects is rather more subtle and flexible than the earlier checklist would suggest. There was a feeling in some of the projects that the initial approach had been too 'evangelical' and that it had not recognised some of the complexities inherent in working with young people:

'I think, probably, very early on the practice was very ideological in terms of pursuing children's rights – that there was no social justice, that nobody listened to children and young people. So there was a real sense of crusade about the project in advocating for young people. It seemed to be a case that everybody out there is bad and we are trying to promote young people's rights and have their voices heard, so we're very righteous.'

Through a process of refinement, these projects have now developed a model of practice that retains young people at the centre of the work, but is also realistic in terms of expectations of others, and of what can be achieved in practice. It is this learning that will be the focus for most of the remainder of the present chapter.

Making contact with young people

The initial contact that projects make with young people is seen as crucial by many of the contributors. Young people who run away have often had bad experiences of adults, including professionals, as illustrated by several research studies (e.g., Stein, Rees and Frost, 1994). Or they may have had no involvement with agencies but have preconceptions about what they might have to offer. The feelings of suspicion, mistrust and disillusionment about adults, which are common among this group of young people, mean that the task of attempting to engage with them requires a considerable amount of skill and tact on the part of project workers. Whether the initial contact was made on the streets, over the telephone, in a drop-in centre, or through a visit to the young person's home, contributors felt that they had very little time to make the right impression with the young person.

The learning from efforts to engage with these young people can be summarised under three broad headings. First, it is seen as being vital to establish the independence of the project from other services, particularly statutory agencies. Second, it is necessary to say something concise and clear to young people about the way the project handles issues of confidentiality. Third, there is a need to emphasise that it is entirely a matter of choice for the young person whether and to what extent they choose to engage with the project:

'You need to be able to tell them who you are, what you are doing, and whether it's optional or not, so they can tell you to get lost. So the things that I make sure I know is our confidentiality policy in bite-size chunks: "We won't tell anyone unless you're in real danger and by that we mean this and this." You don't want to go into your whole confidentiality policy, because what you find is that young people don't often know what confidentiality means. You need to be able to say what you offer.'

It was also seen as important by some contributors doing street work to leave the young person with something tangible – such as some information about the project or something of practical value – in order to create a lasting impression.

Given the short time span of many initial contacts, the above is no easy task, but there was a shared feeling among contributors that this kind of one-to-one contact was essential not only to engage with specific young people but also to promote the work of the project more widely. For most of the projects, word of mouth recommendations were the primary source of publicity.

Advocacy

An advocacy approach to working on the issues raised by young people was seen as a fundamental part of most of the projects' work. In fact, some projects had at times seen their role as being essentially about advocacy. It is important to reflect on the history of the development of work in this area to understand some of the reasons for this, and to appreciate the changes that have occurred over time.

Projects such as Youth Link, Safe in the City and Leeds Safe House were set up more than ten years ago at a time when the concepts of children's rights and young people's participation were not as well established as they are today. The Children Act 1989, which has contributed to the development of more participatory ways of working with young people, did not come into force until October 1991 and the key principles of the Act took some time to be absorbed and incorporated into day-to-day work. There has, in fact, been a shift in professional culture in working with young people over the past decade in both the statutory and voluntary sectors, which needs to be borne in mind in reviewing the early advocacy work undertaken by some of the projects.

Many of the contributors who were involved in this early work now accept, with the wisdom of hindsight, that some of the advocacy work was undertaken with a rather misplaced zeal. There was a tendency to be very adversarial and to push every case as far as possible, without acknowledging the constraints and stresses under which other professionals were working:

> 'Advocacy is not of itself a bad thing, but it depends on how you conduct the advocacy, and if you line up with your basic premise that young people can do no wrong, and say no wrong, then you've got a problem. Then you add to that the moral high ground and the fatally-flawed assumptions that go with that and you take it out and you rather contemptuously parade that in front of everyone with whom you are advocating on behalf of young people then you're probably going to do more harm than good.'

This approach achieved short-term gains for some individual young people, but it also damaged relationships between the projects and other services, and sometimes had an impact on the key relationships in the young person's life.

It may not be useful to dwell on these problems for too long, since the current styles of advocacy undertaken by contributing projects are considerably more subtle. However, there is some important learning from this early experience:

> 'Anybody that's trying to get involved in this kind of work needs to recognise that it's too easy to fall into saying "we're right and you're wrong" – that doesn't get

that young person any further... Although sometimes you have to shout, it's necessary, but it shouldn't be the first port of call, or you will lose goodwill, and this doesn't benefit the young people you work with.'

Lessons from early practice have been absorbed into the current practice of projects. There is still an emphasis on strongly supporting young people in advocating for their desired outcomes. However, this has become tempered by a sensitivity to the restraints with which other professionals are working, and by a recognition of some of the realities of what is achievable in a given situation:

'Having an advocacy model is not that same as just blindly agreeing with everything the young person says, and just saying it again and again more loudly and more angrily to the authority that you're advocating with. There is a balance in terms of how you get across a young person's point of view and how you work with a young person to develop their own point of view that is more sophisticated... If you are advocating with SSD, you have a need for something from them, you need them to put more resources towards that young person – you're asking them to take on board that young person's point of view, and therefore you're in no position to shout the odds... There is an overriding need to stay calm and measured and polite and understand where they're coming from and explain that to the young person, and I think that this can sometimes become lost in the rush to say "this is what this young person wants".'

A second important area for consideration in terms of advocacy work is the extent to which it is an appropriate and useful method of working with all young people who run away. It has already been seen in Chapter 4 that the initial idea of advocacy as a key component of street work at Safe in the City was abandoned as the realities of the situations of young people on the streets became apparent. Advocacy was retained as one component of the project's practice which could be applied in given situations, rather than as an overarching methodology.

This more flexible concept of the place of advocacy in working with young people who run away is also relevant to other models of working. Before its closure, Leeds Safe House was beginning to move away from the idea of advocacy as a core element of service, towards a more flexible approach in which advocacy was one tool available to workers along with others, such as negotiation and mediation, and the Porth Project began to move in that direction before its closure also. A desire for a more flexible range of tools for working with young people was voiced by a number of contributors:

'I think that advocacy can be really useful as part of the toolkit, but I worried about hanging on to that over and above what might help the situation, like negotiation, mediation, compromise – those sorts of things – family support, family therapy, whatever it might be. I don't think you're necessarily disempowering the young person as long as you keep checking out that it's OK with them... [advocacy is] just one role of many that's needed within this sort of crisis, and you've got to step further than that, otherwise it's just too rigid.'

This may seem a rather obvious idea, but it has taken a considerable amount of practice working with young people who run away for projects to develop an understanding of the range of methods needed, and to refine the role of advocacy.

Confidentiality and the handling of information

The issue of confidentiality is absolutely fundamental to discussing approaches to working with young people who run away. Many contributors believe a well-defined and appropriately-framed confidentiality policy is the most important element of good practice in successfully working with young people in this target group:

> 'For me it has always been historically one of the key policy positions that has enabled us to work with detached young people effectively, get alongside them and work with them. But it means that you have to be so rigorous and thorough about that, in your communication of that policy to young people, your partner agencies and the other agencies you are in contact with, in your internal decision-making processes about how and when you do it [breach confidentiality] and how you enact that decision.'

By and large, the projects' thresholds of confidentiality were considerably higher than those in use by many agencies working with young people. Although there was inevitably some variation, there was generally an emphasis on serious and immediate risk as the threshold which needed to be crossed before a breach of confidentiality was considered.

An example of the kind of approach in operation was provided by one contributor:

> 'A good example of that was a 15-year-old female that had alleged physical abuse by her stepdad but didn't want us to do anything with it and at that point was not willing to return home. My feeling was that if we breached confidentiality we stood the risk of losing that young person and of engaging with her... Based on the fact that she was not returning home, we were able not to do anything about it. We had to take everything into account – the nature of the abuse, who else was in the house. As the work progressed and she was planning to return home she understood that at that point we had to breach confidentiality and discuss it with social services. But that was a good example of where the policy worked because we were able to do some really good work with her and I think, had we have gone against her wishes, she wouldn't have engaged again.'

This flexible approach to handling confidentiality when working with specific groups of young people has begun to be accepted as good, and is alluded to in 'Working Together', in relation to working with young people involved in prostitution:

> 'Children involved in prostitution may be difficult to reach, and under very strong pressure to remain in prostitution. They may be fearful of being involved with the police or social services, and may respond best initially to informal contact from health or voluntary sector outreach workers. Gaining the child's trust and confidence is vital if he or she is to be helped to be safe and well, and diverted from prostitution.' (Department of Health, 1999)

The projects contributing to this publication have been at the forefront of the development of this shift in thinking about confidentiality in relation to older children and young people. There is a consensus among contributors that they could not be successful in engaging with the young people with whom they work without a guarantee of a high degree of confidentiality.

Although there is a very strong link between confidentiality and child protection work, several contributors commented on the importance of viewing confidentiality decisions in wider terms than just child protection considerations:

> *'I have become more aware of the need to take a holistic perspective on the risk assessment process; that what we were not just doing was only attending to child protection concerns, which you could interpret in a narrow frame... Is there physical harm, is there sexual abuse or whatever going on here?... The risk there is that you don't factor in the other risks that young people are facing – their mental health, their harmful exposure to drug use...'*

Having a confidentiality policy that is different from the norm places an extra onus on projects to be clear about their policies. Contributors emphasised the need to explain the policy clearly to young people at the outset of the work, to check young people's understanding of the policy, and to provide reminders about it as work progressed. There is a risk that the policy will be interpreted by young people as meaning 100 per cent confidentiality.

One area that perhaps has been paid only limited attention is the notion of young people's competence. The whole basis of the young-person-centred approach and the approach to confidentiality is the notion of young people making their own decisions. However, there are situations where young people may not be able to act in this way. This might be due to extreme pressures exerted upon them by others, or to the state of their mind at that point in time, or due to their maturity of thought. This seems to have been an issue that has been underplayed in projects (although it is included in some projects' procedures), perhaps primarily because it implies some form of assessment of competence which does not sit comfortably with the idea of empowering young people and treating them like adults. However, it may be more of an issue for any project that works with a slightly younger age group or with young people who have difficulties with learning.

There is also a need to put effort into explaining the policy to other agencies, as well as developing agreements and protocols. Projects reported having difficulty at times with other agencies, which could find the approach to confidentiality obstructive or even maverick. Sometimes with agencies, too, there was the misconception that projects would never share information. Contributors had found that it was important to put effort into engaging in a dialogue with other professionals about the policy, so that it was better understood.

For the long-standing projects this was something that happened only after several years of practice:

> *'We have a difficult confidentiality policy for other agencies to comprehend, and my learning from my experience about how you present that is, if you can present it in a way that is not threatening and not questioning other people's professionalism, it is received a lot better... because I've never compromised on the confidentiality of this project, but how it's now received is very different.*

> *'It was explained to other agencies in quite an abrasive manner in the past which, before you even started, made life difficult, because other agencies would receive it in the way that it was given, which was kind of stroppy – "we're not passing on any information about this young person"', etc., – whereas now we still have the same stance, but we have conversations with other agencies about it*

rather than say "this is what we do, good bye". That's made quite a big difference as to how we're received by other agencies.

'I think once they realised that we weren't trying to be particularly precious about everything, but that we were just trying to maintain a service to young people so they at least could talk to us about things, then it was accepted, but that's taken a long time.'

Newer projects had clearly absorbed this learning and spent time explaining their policies to other agencies from the very outset. Provided this was done, contributors felt it was possible to have good working relationships with other agencies applying lower thresholds of confidentiality. Many of the projects had had their approach to confidentiality incorporated into a protocol with statutory agencies, and some (e.g., Safe in the City) had also had the approach endorsed by the local ACPC.

Given the crucial importance of the confidentiality policies for forming good relationships with young people, it is not surprising that many of the contributors commented on the dilemmas involved in making a decision to breach confidentiality against a young person's wishes. These were decisions that projects generally took very seriously, and some had developed specific tools (e.g., checklists or risk assessment forms) or decision-making processes or forums.

Child protection work

The discussion around confidentiality naturally leads to a consideration of child protection work, as many of the confidentiality decisions made by the projects related to child protection issues. Primarily, the projects work with teenagers, and dealing with child protection issues with this age group can be particularly problematic.

Because of their success in engaging with young people and developing a relationship of trust, the projects regularly receive fresh disclosures of abuse and neglect which they feel need to be passed on to statutory agencies. Thus the projects have found it necessary to ensure that their policies and procedures promote a high standard of practice in this area. All projects have in mind clear 'exceptional circumstances' in which they will breach confidentiality because of child protection concerns. These policies have usually been built into service-level agreements and protocols with other agencies.

There are also well-developed procedures for making child protection decisions within projects, with an emphasis on shared decision-making between practitioners and managers. At Safe in the City the decision-making process involves as many members of the team as possible, in order to ensure that different perspectives are included, but it is clearly understood that managers are ultimately responsible and accountable for the decisions made. At projects working outside office hours (e.g., refuges) there are clear procedures for contacting an on-call manager in relation to any child protection concerns that arise. Projects have also developed good procedures for recording child protection decision-making, which include situations where ultimately the decision was taken not to breach confidentiality.

Although there is undoubtedly a high level of expertise and exemplary practice within contributing projects, some concerns were raised by contributors in respect of the approach to child protection. One issue was the level of risk that projects were willing to take in this respect. For example, one contributor felt that Leeds Safe House had gradually lowered its thresholds for passing on child protection concerns, that making child protection referrals had become too routine at the project, and that there was a danger of falling into the trap of making a referral as a means of advocating for the provision of services.

A second concern related to the following-up of child protection referrals. Most of the projects have a short-term focus and work at the young person's initiative. If they lose contact with the young person there is a danger of the child protection issues being allowed to drop. Some contributors felt that, notwithstanding the young-person-centred approach, there should be more follow-up of child protection referrals:

> 'It did feel sometimes as if the child protection referral was a stone that dropped in a pond and sank, after the first few ripples – just sank without trace. It was hard to keep the energy and momentum going to follow it through, particularly because our way of working was very temporary with young people... It felt like a very sporadic responsive service that didn't address things in a very planned way.'

Finally, the substantial amount of child protection work which has been common in projects working with young runaways has considerable implications for the staffing and management of projects, and these are discussed in Chapter 11.

Interactions with families

The approaches to working with families vary quite considerably between contributing projects. Some projects, in particular the street-work projects, have relatively little contact with families because of the nature of the young people with whom they work. Among the projects which commonly work with young people still attached to families, some make a conscious decision to focus work primarily on the young person, whereas others actively seek to engage families in the work that they do. There are strengths and weakness to these approaches which need to be thought through carefully in terms of intended outcomes of the work.

The approach of focusing work primarily or exclusively on the young person has tended to be associated with a strong emphasis on advocacy. As discussed earlier in this chapter, there were strong arguments for diversifying approaches to working with families, including the development of more conciliatory approaches, such as mediation:

> 'We would have a family meeting where the young person wanted that, but what happened with workers – which is almost inevitable, I think – is that they were partial, supporting the young person into that situation, and helping the young person express themselves, which is already valid. But you need to engage the whole family properly. So the family work we were doing wasn't that effective.'

The need for the development of a more flexible approach when working with young people is supported by the suggestions of young people consulted for the 'Still Running' research (Safe on the Streets Research Team, 1999), many of whom identified family support mediation as a service which they felt would have helped their situation:

'Some sort of counselling – maybe where families can go and sort stuff out and stop arguing.' (Safe on the Streets Research Team, 1999)

This idea is also reflected in the direct experience of projects working with these young people:

'One young person said she wanted us to mediate. We said, "We advocate." But she said, "No, I don't want you to advocate, I want you to mediate, because I'm wrong as well."'

This is a particularly important area for future development of practice. There are strengths inherent in the advocacy approach (particularly when working with young people in care or in the child protection arena) which have enabled projects to engage successfully with young people. There may also be some cases where this approach is helpful when working with families. However, in the field of family work there is a need to pilot and evaluate alternative approaches to resolving the issues which young people bring to projects and for some flexibility to be built into models of working to cater for the diversity of needs of young people who run away.

Issues of long-term engagement versus crisis intervention

As has already been discussed in the preceding chapters on models of working, most of the projects saw their role as including an element of crisis intervention. For most projects the concept of a crisis was applied to an individual incident of running away, and this was seen as an opportunity to engage with young people (and sometimes their families) on problematic issues which underpinned running away. For the street-work projects, the concept of crisis could also be applied to events which disrupted young people's established survival strategies on the streets, and perhaps offered an opportunity to promote alternative solutions, including moving off the streets.

One of the problems of the projects' successes in working with young people is that young people do not always share this desire to limit their involvement to a short-term crisis intervention. In the experience of contributors, some young people feel they have been listened to and taken seriously for the first time, and are reluctant to lose the relationship they have built up with the project, or with individual workers:

'I think it was confusing. Refuge was seen as a short-term intervention and yet the young people's need was for longer-term, particularly emotional, support. There was always a tension in the work between those two things.'

This reluctance is compounded by the difficulties which the projects often experienced in trying to refer young people on to longer-term support services (see also Chapter 6).

There is therefore a tension between the concept of short-term crisis intervention on the one hand, and the desires of young people and realities of disengaging with them on the other hand. For example, in refuge projects, the limitations on follow-up work with young people often led to young people coming back into refuge for repeat stays in order to get access to the services they felt they needed.

The reality is that most of the established projects contributing to this study have become engaged with some young people either sporadically or continuously for several years. This was an issue which was raised in a study of four projects in the mid-1990s (Stein, Rees and Frost, 1994) but which has still not been fully resolved. For example, while Leeds Safe House ended up working with some young people regularly for two or three years, the practice model remained short-term focused. There was a tendency to focus on immediate issues on each occasion that the young person came into refuge, and there was little sense of a long-term plan to the work. In some cases the project appears to have been adhering to an idea of how to conduct its work that was not in tune with the realities of young people's lives and their need for some form of continuous independent support.

An example of this was the way the project dealt with child protection issues, as discussed earlier in the chapter, but is also was reflected in other kinds of work:

> 'We responded to need, or we tried to, and that was great but there wasn't the follow-through and I don't think other people were clear about what we were doing and where it began and ended. So we might go into a school with a young person and talk about problems that they were having there and make a lot of agreements, and then the young person might leave refuge and we'd never see them again or talk to those people in that school again.'

There is an important debate to be had about the extent to which the potential for long-term involvement should be taken into account when planning services, and this issue needs careful consideration when setting up projects working with young people who run away. While many young people's situations are suited to a short-term crisis intervention model, there are some circumstances where this will have little or no value. Should the project take on long-term work with these young people? Are there other services in the area which could fulfil this function? What implications do the answers to these questions have for the allocation of resources within the project?

Key points

- A young-person-centred approach has proved effective in engaging with young people who run away. However, it needs to be realistic rather than 'evangelical' in order to effectively move work forward and it needs to work in partnership with other agencies.

- Techniques for making contact with young people who run away require an emphasis on clarity, directness and the independence of the service, in order to establish some trust with young people who have often felt let down by adults.

- An advocacy approach can in certain circumstances be a vital element of working with young people who run away – for example, where there are child protection issues or issues relating to the quality of statutory service provision. However, projects need to guard against the indiscriminate use of advocacy combined with an over-zealous advocacy style which created problems for the early projects working with young runaways.

- The issue of confidentiality is vital to the development of work with young people who run away. Traditionally, projects in this field have worked to a high threshold of confidentiality and this approach has recently been endorsed in official guidance. Effort needs to be put into ensuring that young people and other professionals are clear about the approach to confidentiality.

■ Projects working with young runaways will regularly have to deal with child protection concerns. Existing projects have developed a high level of expertise in this area and it is vital that any new projects that are developed give this issue priority consideration. This should include the development of understandings and agreements with statutory agencies concerning the approach to handling child protection issues.

■ A more flexible range of models of intervention needs to be developed to work with young people and their families. Existing models have primarily focused on individual work with young people, yet most of the reasons for running away relate to problems within the family.

■ Many young people who run away have long-standing problems in one or more areas of their lives. The short-term crisis intervention undertaken by most existing projects can be effective in resolving immediate issues, but there is also a need to attend to the longer-term support needs of young people and families, either through the provision of ongoing support or through effective referral to other agencies. If this is not achieved there is a danger of projects becoming caught up in a cyclical crisis-driven pattern of working with some young people.

9

INTER-AGENCY WORKING

Working together in partnership with other agencies has, in recent years, received increasing emphasis as an essential aspect of good practice in the social welfare field. In view of this, some of the issues which projects face in working in partnership are no different from those being grappled with on a wider level within organisations working in many different fields. However, as will have become clear in the previous chapter, there are specific dynamics involved in the process of working with young people who run away which may make inter-agency working particularly difficult. This chapter pulls together contributors' comments about these issues, together with some of the solutions that projects have developed in order to maintain workable relationships.

Tensions in inter-agency working

Given the nature of the work and the approaches taken by the projects described in this report, a certain amount of tension with other agencies is seemingly inevitable. For some, the act of setting up a project in a specific locality can be interpreted as a 'thinly-veiled criticism' of existing provision (particularly by statutory services) in the area. Certainly this seems to have been an issue both for Leeds Safe House and the Porth Project in their early years, although there may be lessons to be learned here about the way such projects are set up:

> 'When I look back in terms of refuge, it seemed to be that The Children's Society, for whatever reason, took a decision in isolation to situate its refuge in Leeds and while there was initial discussions to say that "this is what we are doing"… Maybe you couldn't really do more at the time because there was a need for The Children's Society not only to develop a service delivery, a practice model, but it was also in the situation of highlighting an issue and a need which may not have been easily acknowledged or welcomed.'

Beyond this developmental issue, there are various aspects to the approaches taken by projects which can potentially create problems in working with other agencies.

The young-person-centred approach taken by projects can create a rift with statutory agencies in particular, and the stance on confidentiality can be seen as maverick or irresponsible:

> 'There is a tension there, in that the statutory services can sometimes look at the voluntary sector or look at somebody that works with a higher threshold [of confidentiality] and see that as very unprofessional, because the professional standards are often perceived to belong to the statutory services, and having a

policy that means you step out a bit and are able to work with young people a bit longer also means that it's going to bring [you] into conflict... So the challenge for any project working to a higher threshold is, "Can your own organisation live with it?", "Can the workers live with it?" – because that may be a choice about whether they work here or not.'

Moreover, the use of advocacy as a standard practice tool is prone to create adversarial and antagonistic relationships with other professionals:

'By doing advocacy with young people you find that you're viewed as antagonistic by others, whether that be agencies or parents or carers... It puts you into conflict, being seen as do-gooders, maverick people.'

This is especially true when the purposes of advocacy and the roles of workers are not clearly understood:

'I think it can work but you've got to be able to distinguish very clearly what the advocate's role is. Quite often the approach of other professionals would be appealing as an adult or as a professional, but you're there in an advocacy role and essentially you're an extension of the young person and their opinion. You're not putting across a professional opinion there and I'm not sure that that was always clear, either from the person from the other side of that [the social services], or even for the person providing it.'

A further tension for refuge-based projects stems from their legal exemptions. This means that they can allow a young person to stay for 14 days without the consent of parents or carers, including the local authority, where relevant. This creates a power imbalance in discussions with social services staff which may not be conducive to positive joint working.

The voluntary sector also sees its role as being to advocate and campaign for children and young people collectively, as well as individually. Again, if not carefully handled, this kind of activity runs the risk of alienating professionals who may feel directly or indirectly criticised.

All these factors militate against the creation and maintenance of positive working relationships between projects and the statutory sector. Certainly, the early histories of the first wave of projects working with missing young people reflected these issues. There were often major rifts and tensions between these projects and the local Social Services Department (SSD) in particular, stemming from all the above factors, but especially from the over-enthusiastic use of advocacy, as discussed in Chapter 8.

Yet, more recently, these older projects have succeeded in establishing far better relationships with statutory services. In addition, the newer projects that have been set up seem, by and large, to have avoided these problems and to have had good working relationships with local networks of agencies from the outset. This may be partly due to a gradual shift in professional culture towards a greater acceptance of young people's participation, as discussed in the introductory chapter:

'The methodologies require services to be accessible to these very detached young people and therefore the key issue for them is confidentiality, because it's about power and control, and power is the problem with all these types of services. The cultural shift is such that having young people's wishes and feelings at the centre of planning of services and of initiatives is now enshrined in the way in

which government documentation and legislation is formulated. So maybe we need to be fighting a different battle now.'

However, there are a number of other explanatory factors evident in the accounts of contributors, which are discussed in the second half of this chapter.

Despite these positive developments, significant tensions are likely to remain between projects working with young people who run away and other agencies, particularly SSDs. These stem from difficulties the projects often experience in assisting young people in gaining access to services and resources. This was an issue which prompted substantial comment from contributors.

Ironically, despite concerns about the level of confidentiality with which the projects operate, and the impact this might have on child protection decisions, many contributors commented on the difficulty of taking a child protection route with the young people with whom they worked. There seems to be widespread reluctance on the part of social services to accept child protection concerns in relation to older young people who run away. One contributor recounted the case of a 13-year-old girl living at home who was taking heroin and who was not seen as being at enough risk to be accommodated by the local authority. The issue of lack of access to statutory resources creates huge frustration for staff within projects, although it is recognised that social services have limited resources and that, in terms of child protection work, younger children tend to be prioritised over teenagers:

> *'When you engage with a young person, a whole range of issues emerge for that young person apart from the running away. And one of the difficulites is, how do you begin to address those issues? If you are reliant, for instance, on statutory agencies, then you may not be able to address those issues quickly – because we find that we don't get a particularly quick response, for instance, around child protection issues for teenagers, and on the one hand you can understand that. If you're needing to deal with babies with broken legs or teenagers, then people do prioritise – that may not be right but it's a reality of the situation at present.'*

However, there was also a recognition that child protection procedures may not always be a helpful or appropriate way of working with young people who run away:

> *'Sometimes, what you would think automatically would be a child protection issue doesn't always have a child protection response from social services; but that in itself isn't a bad thing because a child protection response might not be the best way forward for these young people. Child protection procedures can be quite traumatic – it might not be what they need.'*

Before moving on to look at the factors facilitating good inter-agency relationships, one further comment on inter-agency working relates to the failure on the part of a number of projects to create adequate networks with other local agencies. This seems to have been a particular problem for refuge projects, as discussed in Chapter 3, but there have also been concerns about insularity within other projects at certain points in their development. There is a risk that this insularity will, in the long run, be detrimental both to the project and, more importantly, to young people.

Factors facilitating relationships with other agencies

Informing and consulting other agencies in the early developmental stages of a project

Projects working with young people who run away can be seen by other agencies as quite threatening. As pointed out earlier, the very act of setting up a service can be interpreted as an implied criticism of existing services for young people. In order to counteract negative consequences of this, it is vital to involve local agencies from the very early developmental stages. When Leeds Safe House was set up, this did not happen:

> 'Social services weren't that happy at not being consulted about refuge being plonked in Leeds in the first place. In starting out with any piece of work, one of the initial things that you should always do is to identify who the key stakeholders are before engaging in developing it any further, that purely in principle they are supportive for this piece of work, or even if they are not supportive it has got a mandate from somebody that it has to be provided, whether that be from central government or individual local authorities or whatever.'

As a consequence of this it was always difficult for the project to work effectively in partnership and there was a sense of lost opportunity:

> 'I think it was one of the brilliant things about being a voluntary and independent organisation that we had freedoms to work with young people in quite fresh, innovative ways. And one of the great losses, because we didn't set ourselves up in partnership with other agencies from the beginning, was that we weren't able to realise the potential that we had as an organisation that young people actually trusted.'

On the other hand, the Bournemouth refuge had better relationships with local agencies from the outset, and this continued throughout the history of the project:

> 'I have a view that how things start does affect how they develop. It's very difficult if you've had a slightly difficult start to put things right down the line. There were some very sympathetic people in the police and social services to start with. We had good protocols. We had some horrendous cases, but it was OK, I didn't get the feeling ever that there was any antipathy.'

More recently the development of the flexible refuge by the South Coast Runaways Initiative, as discussed in Chapter 6, has been undertaken with the close involvement of police and social services:

> 'The idea came about and then we decided to meet with social services to put it to them – you know, "This is an idea we've had, what do you think? What we want to do is to negotiate a protocol with you around this." And they said, "That's fine, this is who you need to contact", and it went very well. You've got to have a relationship with statutory partners. It doesn't mean we're not in a position to challenge them. We challenge social services every day... But we can still have a dialogue at another level with managers and improve the way the whole system here works with young people.'

Developing services on the basis of locally identified need

Historically, there has been a fair amount of resistance to accepting the widespread and serious nature of young people running away. Early research studies spent a considerable amount of energy in producing evidence of the level of need, often in the face of denial from other professionals.

One of the reasons for the success of the ASTRA Project in Gloucester (described in Chapter 5) seems to have been an awareness and acceptance among local agencies in the city of the importance of the issue of young people running away, and a shared desire to tackle this issue. The same is true for the two missing persons schemes set up by Barnardo's in West Yorkshire (also described in Chapter 5).

Thus, where it is possible, projects should aim to build on locally-held concerns about young people running away. Where this is not possible, it may be necessary to undertake research or audit activities in partnership with local agencies in order to produce locally-based evidence which is accepted as credible and relevant. This is an approach which Safe in the City has utilised in Manchester. The project played a key role in commissioning a research study which emphasised a participatory form of enquiry. This study was successful in creating a receptive culture for debate about the needs of young people on the streets in the city. More recently, the project has been undertaking a study of the needs of black young people with the aim of developing locally-based responses to their needs (see Chapter 10 for more details).

Involving agencies in a steering group

The second way in which projects have been successful in building bridges with other local agencies is through the creation of a steering group with representatives of local agencies. This provides a forum for discussing issues arising out of the project's work, and also means that the representatives can become 'champions' of the project within their own agency, thus promoting a more positive image. It is interesting that the Bradford Young Missing Persons Scheme emerged from the steering group set up in relation to another project.

Putting resources into clarifying the project's policies and approach

For the longer-established projects, some of the initial problems with other agencies seemed to have been created by a misunderstanding of what the project did or what it aimed to achieve. The approach to confidentiality and child protection was often a particular area for confusion, and it was only through a concerted effort to explain the approach that projects succeeded in improving relationships. Again, with newer projects, these lessons seem to have been absorbed, with contributors emphasising the value of making visits to relevant agencies from the outset of the project's development in order to share information:

> '*When I first started, one of the first things that I did was go around and actually speak to all the relevant local agencies and with as many as possible I went around and did it face to face, rather than send a leaflet around saying "this is now in existence". And I asked if I could go to team meetings and talk to workers and explain what I do. I go in and explain our confidentiality policy so that you don't get caught into the myth [of] "Don't talk to [the project] because they won't talk to anybody, they've got such a tight confidentiality policy."*'

Along with this there is a need to be clear about the roles of the different professionals within multi-agency forums:

> 'The critical thing is an understanding of role, which I think was an issue for a lot of the projects in their early days – that that wasn't clear. So if you're taking on the role as advocate for a young person there's got to be a clear definition of advocacy, there's got to be an understanding of your [advocacy] role in that, and very clear distinction between that and the [social work] capacity. Because that's where I think there have been difficulties and I think what has been very hard to swallow as a result of all that is the negative effects that has had on young people.'

A realistic approach

The fifth factor promoting more positive relationships with other agencies has been a gradual refinement of approaches to advocacy in particular, which are discussed further in Chapter 8. This has entailed developing a recognition of the constraints with which other organisations are faced, and adopting a more subtle and realistic approach to attempting to assist young people in achieving their desired outcomes.

Sharing knowledge and expertise with other projects

A number of contributing projects have developed initiatives to share knowledge and expertise with other local agencies. One of the forms this has taken has been to assist other projects in developing their practice with under-16s. There is often an element of fear in working with this target group, particularly from smaller voluntary agencies that work mainly with young people in an older age group. This fear is often born out of a lack of knowledge about the legalities of working with young people under 16, including issues of parental consent, and about the child protection system. Several projects (including the Breaking Free Project and Safe in the City) have therefore provided information to other local agencies with which they have developed links, and supported them in developing their practice with this age group:

> 'We've worked quite hard with them… We've helped them write an under-16s policy so that they now feel really confident that if someone who is under 16 comes in that they would know how to deal with it, what to do, who to contact. They feel clearer about their responsibilities under the Children Act, they've got a really sound policy now.'

Several projects have also been involved in developing local protocols around working with young people who run away, in partnership with social services and the police. One of these is the Kirklees SOS Scheme, which also undertakes partnership working on individual cases with social workers, where appropriate:

> 'We have got quite a few referrals from social services as well, and what we also offer to social services is more a consultative role… if the social worker or family support team have got a very good working relationship with a young person, it's not always helpful that we also work with that young person, but we have resources we can offer them, ideas about young people going missing. We offer that service as well, which has had quite a high take-up and has been quite successful with work carried out with young people.'

Through the above means, projects working with young people who run away have been able to forge positive relationships with statutory agencies within their local areas. It is important to note that this has been achieved without a substantial change in approaches to working with young people on the part of the projects.

Key points

- Projects working with young people who run away face an inherently difficult task in establishing and maintaining positive and constructive relationships with other agencies. These difficulties stem from several factors:
  - The establishment of a project for runaways can be perceived by statutory services as a criticism of service provision
  - The young-person-centred and advocacy approaches often adopted by projects are, in the view of many contributors, an inevitable source of conflict
  - The approach to confidentiality can be perceived as maverick or irresponsible
  - For refuges, the legal exemptions granted to projects can be a source of frustration and resentment within social services
  - The resource shortage faced by statutory services can often lead to conflict with projects attempting to get access to services for young people.

- Projects working with young runaways therefore will need to put considerable energy into inter-agency relationships. The experience of contributing projects suggests that if there is a commitment to this, then it is possible to have positive, or at least workable relationships with other agencies. The key elements which contributors identified as being helpful in this respect are:
  - Informing and consulting agencies in the early developmental stages of a project
  - Developing services on the basis of locally-held concerns or local evidence of need
  - Involving agencies in a steering group
  - Clarifying project philosophy and policies
  - Developing a pragmatic approach with realistic expectations of other agencies
  - Sharing knowledge and expertise with others.

10

WORKING WITH DIVERSITY

There has been a gradual development of awareness within projects working with young runaways that their services are not reaching out equally to all sections of the target group, and are not always successful in adequately meeting the diverse needs of the young people with whom they have contact. This chapter looks at the approaches which projects have developed to tackle these issues. It also examines some of the ways in which anti-discriminatory practice with this target group might be undertaken in the future.

The development of interventions with young people who have run away over the past two decades was spurred initially by perceived needs in the West End of London, and this was followed by a gradual diversification geographically, and in terms of working methods, as outlined in Chapter 1. A drawback of this approach is that responses based on visible need will not adequately address the needs of all members of the target group. More recently, research has highlighted some of the specific issues facing young people from certain sub-groups within the overall population of young people who run away, but the picture painted by this evidence is still incomplete.

Before embarking on a discussion of the issues in terms of minority groups, it is worth noting that, in terms of gender mix, the various practice models have generally been fairly evenly used. Research suggests that females are slightly more likely to run away than males (Safe on the Streets Research Team, 1999) and this pattern has often been apparent in project usage.

This chapter looks first at the issue of working with young people from black and minority ethnic groups. This is the area of anti-discriminatory practice where there is most research evidence and practice experience. Later in the chapter, the comments of contributors on other aspects of anti-discriminatory practice – including working with lesbian, gay and bisexual young people, and disabled young people – are presented.

Working with black young people

In the context of the discussion below, the term 'black' is used to include young people of African, Caribbean and Asian origin. However, there are some significant differences between sub-groups of black young people and a distinction is made where appropriate between young people of African-Caribbean origin and those of Indian/Pakistani/Bangladeshi origin. This distinction is itself an over-simplification as there is considerable diversity within these sub-groups, but is helpful in defining some of the broad issues.

Before discussing practice issues, it is relevant briefly to review existing knowledge on patterns of running away among young people from different cultural backgrounds.

Evidence from research

As shown in Chapter 2, there is evidence of differing rates of running away among young people from different ethnic groups, with black young people being somewhat less likely to run away than white young people (Safe on the Streets Research Team, 1999). However, the estimated rates of running away (7.5 per cent for young people of African-Caribbean origin and 5.5 per cent for young people of Indian/Pakistani/Bangladeshi origin, compared with over 10 per cent for white young people) still represent a significant incidence of running away under the age of 16.

There are surprisingly few ethnic differences in patterns of running away. There are no significant differences between young people from the three main ethnic groups (white, African-Caribbean, and Indian/Pakistani/Bangladeshi) in terms of the age at which they first ran away, the number of times they had run away, the proportion who classified themselves as having been forced to leave rather than having run away, the likelihood of sleeping rough, or in how far they travelled while they were away. The only significant difference in running away patterns is the finding that black young people are likely to stay away longer than white young people when they do run away.

Broadly speaking, reasons for running away appear to be the same for young people in all ethnic groups including high levels of conflict, physical abuse, emotional abuse and neglect. However, for young people of Indian/Pakistani/Bangladeshi origin, there are additional cultural factors. It is vital that professionals understand if services are to be culturally sensitive.

Although it is dangerous to make generalisations, many young people of Indian/Pakistani/Bangladeshi origin grow up in relatively traditional, close-knit communities with a very specific set of cultural norms. There will often be considerable pressure on families and young people within these communities to conform. The incidence of a young person, particularly a young woman, running away can be seen as a failure on the part of her or his family, and this can have dramatic repercussions in terms of stigmatisation of the young person and the family. For a young person living in this cultural context, the decision to run away can therefore be a much more serious and far-reaching one than for other young people, and the use of services can exacerbate the situation:

> *'One of the dangers of refuge is that, having brought young people into refuge, the fragile ties they might have had which might have been the road home, could be irrevocably broken, particularly within some cultures, like the quite understandable distress expressed by the Asian community about [young people] living in a mixed refuge where proper attention wasn't given to their cultural needs – and I think that that was a well-founded criticism.'*

The implications of this fact for the development of services aimed at meeting these young people's needs is discussed later in this chapter.

Finally, in this brief overview, qualitative research indicates that there may be some other significant differences in the experiences of young people after running away. Black young people are unlikely to be visibly on the streets when they run away because of fear of racism or harassment. They may also find that agencies they approach are not always sensitive to or geared to catering for their needs (Safe on the Streets Research Team, 1999). They are therefore more likely be invisible and to rely on support networks within their own communities. Again, this has implications for developing services designed to meet these needs.

Access to existing services

As discussed in earlier chapters, each model of work developed with young people who run away has been primarily successful at engaging with a particular sub-group of the target population. There have been concerns in projects operating each practice model about the extent to which they have been accessible to a range of young people.

The evidence on this issue varies according to the practice model. There does seem to have been a tendency for city-centre-based street-work projects to work primarily with white young people. As discussed above, black young people who run away are unlikely to find the city centre a safe environment, so a city-centre-based model is, by definition, unlikely to engage effectively with young people from minority ethnic groups. However, there are young people from these groups sleeping rough outside city centres.

Turning to other practice models, monitoring statistics of project usage gathered over a nine-year period at Leeds Safe House do not suggest that the project was under-used by young people from minority ethnic groups, based on estimates of running away rates from research. Thus there is no evidence of a lack of access in this case, but there are other issues in relation to service delivery and anti-discriminatory practice, which are discussed later in the chapter.

In missing persons schemes there has been some concern about the effectiveness of this model of working in relation to young people from ethnic minorities. The projects attempt to make contact with all young people reported missing. However, there are some suggestions that young people from particular cultural backgrounds may be less likely to be reported as missing by parents or carers. Contributors also mentioned experience some gate-keeping by parents when attempting to make contact with young people of Asian origin, although to date the numbers of such referrals have been small, so the evidence on this matter is not conclusive.

Developing more inclusive practice models

The issue of uneven access to existing services can be tackled in two ways: through measures that promote more equal access, and through the development of different services that might better meet the needs of specific target groups.

In terms of increasing access to existing services, projects have attempted a number of strategies, including developing better links with organisations working with minority ethnic groups and with communities, and improving publicity in order to be more culturally inclusive. For projects relying on face-to-face initial contact with young people, the composition of the staff team can also influence access rates. Youth Link has noticed an increase in the numbers of black young people on the streets in the city centre, particularly during the day. Monitoring figures have suggested that when the street work pair includes a black worker, the level of contact with these black young people is higher. Consequently the project has created a specific post within the street-work team to attempt to increase its contact with these young people.

Although such measures are vital in ensuring equality of access to existing services, they cannot alter the extent to which models of working may not be suited to the needs of particular groups of young people. A wider range of services should therefore be developed to meet the diversity of need.

An example of this approach is provided by Safe in the City. In response to the low usage of its Manchester city-centre services by black young people running away, the project created a specific team to work with this target group. The team's work is still at a developmental stage. Research has been carried out into the local issues for black young people running away, primarily focusing on young people of African-Caribbean origin. This supports the above research findings in relation to issues of harassment and racism directed at black young people on the streets and the consequent reliance on local community networks. The team has spent a lot of time networking with agencies working with black young people throughout the city, and aims to develop a community-based model of work which attaches services to existing agencies and projects that are already engaged with this target group.

A similar approach is likely to be needed in order to devise culturally sensitive services for young people of Indian/Pakistani/Bangladeshi origin. Safe on the Streets – Leeds is currently undertaking research in West Yorkshire into the needs of these young people in relation to running away. Given the discussion above about specific cultural issues for this group, it is evident that many existing practice models are not appropriate to their needs. In the view of one contributor there is a particular need for preventive community-based work with young people of Indian/Pakistani/ Bangladeshi origin. This is necessary because the consequences of running away can be so far-reaching.

There is also a need to develop approaches to working with young people and families that are more rooted in the specific cultural context. The advocacy approach practised at Leeds Safe House, for example, together with the provision of accommodation without parental consent, often ran the risk of making things worse for young people. Mediation approaches would seem to be a more appropriate strategy for resolving the issues faced by young people. It may also be possible to provide respite accommodation with parental consent, using the model developed by the Home & Away Project (see Chapter 6).

> *'I think if there was a project that was developed in relation to providing specific family mediation work with young people and a retreat, I think that would work, if it's done in conjunction with families [i.e., a respite facility that the family could agree to].'*

It may also be possible to provide respite accommodation with parental consent, using the model developed by the Home & Away Project (see Chapter 6).

Service delivery issues

The issue of language has been a significant issue for a number of the projects. Although young people are usually able to speak English, their parents and other family members may not. Several projects which make initial contact with families by written means have developed information in relevant languages. However, people may not always be literate in languages they speak, and verbal approaches may be a more effective means of communication.

Young people who run away often have essential practical needs such as food and hygiene products. Catering for these needs can be a prerequisite to engaging with young people on the streets or in accommodation-based projects. It is vital that projects ensure that the practical help they provide is sensitive to the different cultural needs young people may have. This might include carrying a range of skin-care products while working on the streets, offering a range of food for young people in refuge, and so on. This is a very basic area which contributors felt had not always been attended to fully in projects in the past.

There are also issues around developing cultural competence in order to provide culturally-sensitive and appropriate services to young people whatever their background:

> *'I think [when] working with Asian young people we got very uncertain and worried and perhaps didn't take enough steps to learn about the community the young person had come from, and the best ways to negotiate and mediate with people in that young person's community.'*

This points to the need for effective training and staff development opportunities, as discussed later.

Working with young people from other minority groups

The picture in terms of usage of projects by minority groups other than black young people is less clear. In terms of lesbian, gay and bisexual young people, recent UK research has not found a clear link between issues of sexuality and young people running away. However, there have been methodological difficulties in terms of this issue. Safe on the Streets – Leeds is currently undertaking research specifically into the issue of lesbian, gay and bisexual young people running away which will hopefully throw further light on this issue.

There have been a number of specific initiatives within projects in relation to working with lesbian, gay and bisexual young people. In its early years a substantial amount of Youth Link's work was with gay young men in Birmingham city centre. This was partly related to characteristics of the local situation, but the project also had a sexual health worker, seconded from a health authority, and this may have promoted issues of sexuality within the work. Leeds Safe House employed a specialist worker to focus on lesbian, gay and bisexual issues but there were barriers preventing this worker from spending sufficient time focusing on these issues (see discussion later in the chapter). Safe in the City ran a group for gay young men on the streets in Manchester city centre, in partnership with two other street agencies (a mental health project and a youth homelessness/empowerment project). The aim of this initiative was to facilitate mutual support between the young people. Finally, the Breaking Free Project has worked with a number of young women who have had issues in relation to sexuality. The project has produced leaflets, based on ones developed in Canada, giving straightforward information about sexuality and offering suggestions about where to go for support and further information.

However, as one contributor commented, grappling with the issue of sexuality is quite difficult because people's identities are not necessarily visible. There was therefore a feeling amongst contributors that whilst some positive steps had been taken, there was a need for further development of understanding and expertise in relation to issues of sexuality:

> *'I think that young people whose sexuality was in question sometimes we were very affirming of that but also sometimes we got a bit confused because so many young people who came in had been damaged, their sexuality had been damaged by the different kinds of abuse, whether it was sexual abuse or damage to their self-esteem through other kinds of abuse... I think we got muddled sometimes and didn't know how to treat a young person who is damaged sexually and how to differentiate between that and a young person struggling to find their sexuality.'*

Turning to the issue of disability, the barriers presented by specific service models were highlighted in Stein, Rees and Frost (1994). The emphasis on telephone access to refuges, and the focus on city-centre street work both reduce the likelihood of working with young people with disabilities. So far, there has been relatively little specific development in relation to the issues of disabled young people who run away, in terms of either research or practice. Exceptions to this are two practice developments at Youth Link. The project has made efforts to ensure that it produces information which is accessible to young people who have difficulties with reading, and has purchased a software package to incorporate Widgit (a symbolic language) into publicity and other materials. Youth Link's Internet service (described in Chapter 7) is also seen as a means of offering a service which may be accessible to young people who are not able to contact the project via the telephone.

General anti-discriminatory issues

Contributors also commented on the need for a focus on anti-discriminatory practice within the wider organisation and management of projects. Many of the points made here have a wider relevance than just in relation to working with young people who run away.

Project development

Given the discussion above about the inappropriateness of certain practice models for engaging with particular sub-groups of young people, it is clear that thinking about anti-discriminatory practice should be built into the planning and early development of projects. As one contributor pointed out, if this is not done at this stage, practice can become inflexible and it can be very difficult to bring about changes later.

As discussed earlier, this planning should include information-gathering and the building of links with a range of local organisations working with minority groups.

Staffing

There are a number of recruitment and staffing issues which need to be considered in terms of working with young people who run away. The issue of qualifications and recruitment is discussed in Chapter 11.

A key issue discussed by several contributors related to the advantages and disadvantages of employing specialist staff. A number of projects have employed staff specifically to focus on issues of ethnicity or sexuality, and Safe in the City has developed a black young people's team. This can be a useful strategy for ensuring that anti-discriminatory issues are adequately addressed within projects. However, there can also be a danger of seeing these staff as the experts on certain issues and, therefore, not take a more general responsibility for anti-discriminatory practice. In addition, where specialist workers are employed partly to do face-to-face work with young people, it can be difficult for them to find the time to develop other aspects of their work appropriately, given the crisis-driven nature of much work with young people who run away.

Irrespective of the decisions a project makes about creating specialist posts, there is also a need to develop the cultural competence of the whole staff team, including training, secondment opportunities, and the provision of a range of literature which staff can access in order to develop their understanding and practice. The role of supervision is also vital in ensuring that anti-discriminatory issues are kept on the agenda.

Policy and practice

There are specific areas of project policy that require careful thinking in terms of anti-discriminatory practice. A particular area of focus should be policies on child protection. There is a risk of decisions on child protection issues being made on the basis of a set of dominant cultural assumptions which do not apply to all young people. While this is an issue that can apply to any agency working with children and young people, the high profile of child protection issues within work with young people who run away makes it a particularly important issue in the context of this report. Again, then, there is a need to develop the cultural competence of staff teams, but also there is a need to build checks and balances into the decision-making process, and also to review decisions at a later date in order to learn from practice.

On a more general note, one contributor summed up the development of good-quality anti-discriminatory practice with young people who run away as incorporating two principles: transparency and choice. Projects need to give out clear, accessible information to all young people about what they can offer and about their policies and practice. This needs to happen in terms of both publicity and awareness-raising, and once the young person has made initial contact with the project. Young people should also be given choice about how to engage with the project. This should include as many different avenues as possible to access services, and choices about who they work with at the project. Consideration should always be given to offering a range of workers (e.g., mixed street-work pairs) but it should not be assumed that a person from a particular background or group will necessarily want to engage with a worker from that group.

Key points

- Research suggests that while there are many similarities in reasons for running away among young people from different ethnic groups, there are also some key differences in terms of the cultural context, particularly for young people of Indian/Pakistani/Bangladeshi origin.

- Research also indicates that young people from black and ethnic minority groups are less likely to be visible when they run away.

■ The above factors mean that services need to be sensitive to cultural differences, and that more inclusive practice models should be developed in order to meet the needs of young people from minority ethnic backgrounds. Approaches that are effective in working with white young people who run away are often not easily transferrable to different cultural contexts.

■ The development of practice in relation to lesbian, gay and bisexual young people who run away has been limited to date, and more attention should be paid to this issue in future.

■ A similar remark applies to working with disabled young people, where issues such as access to services have not been extensively addressed to date.

■ There is also a need carefully to consider anti-discriminatory issues in terms of the general development and management of projects working with young people who run away. This includes the need to keep issues of diversity and cultural competence at the forefront in terms of the recruitment and training of staff, and the need to consider the anti-discriminatory implication of policies and practice in relation to areas such as child protection and general service delivery.

11

STAFFING AND MANAGEMENT

This chapter looks at the issues involved for managers and staff working in projects with young people who run away. The focus here is on issues that are specific to working in this field, rather than on general learning about good practice in management and staffing. However, the messages contained in this chapter are still likely to be of relevance to other fields of work which involve engaging with disadvantaged and/or detached target groups.

Recruitment of staff

The recruitment of staff to work with young people who run away presents some difficult dilemmas for organisations and managers. Judging by the comments of many of the contributors, there is an ongoing debate between the need for qualified staff (and in particular staff with social work qualifications) and the need for staff who can engage with young people in innovative ways and in unusual settings:

> 'We appoint and recruit people who do not easily adapt well to managerial structures and managerial oversight... it's striking that balance, really, to have good enough management to be confident that your quality of work, your standard of work is there, but sufficient leeway to allow people room to manoeuvre and operate – because you're sending two staff out on a night-time at eight o'clock, and they're on their own and they've got to be enabled and empowered to behave and operate effectively on their own, make decisions there and then.'

Most, but by no means all, practice staff in the projects contributing to this report held a qualification in either youth and community work or social work. There is also a debate about the relative merits of employing workers from youth work and social work backgrounds for this kind of work.

These debates stem from the approaches to working that have been developed with this target group of young people, discussed in depth in Chapter 8. In summary, there is an emphasis on working in a young-person-centred way in order to engage successfully with the young people but, given their background and situations, also a need regularly to handle issues of confidentiality and child protection.

However, it is interesting to note that one contributor from a statutory background found it necessary to go through a process of adjustment to the approach to confidentiality and child protection in operation at one of the projects.

There is no simple answer to the above debates, and no consensus between contributors about what is the best approach. It seems important that managers, and others responsible for developing projects, should be aware of the need for careful consideration of a balance of skills and competencies within the team. It may be, for example, that a lack of statutory background at practitioner level can be balanced by substantial experience at senior practitioner/managerial level. There is also likely to be a need for good training and preparation of all new staff, whatever their background, in handling child protection issues with this particular target group.

The above debate also has a relevance in terms of anti-discriminatory practice. Several projects reported difficulties in recruiting qualified staff. There is a general skills shortage, but this seems to be more marked in relation to the shortage of qualified staff from minority ethnic backgrounds. A consequence of requiring qualifications may be a failure to recruit a staff team who are diverse in terms of cultural background, and this will have a knock-on effect on other issues, as discussed in Chapter 10.

Composition of teams

One aspect of the composition of teams – the profile of qualifications – has already been discussed above. Other comments made by contributors relate to the extent of specialisation that might be necessary or helpful in order to deliver services to young people who run away. This is likely to be most relevant for projects working with a diverse user group and wanting to offer a range of approaches to meet differing needs – for example, advocacy, family mediation, counselling, and so on. Some contributors felt that it would not be possible for each member of staff to be competent in and comfortable with all the different approaches that might be necessary:

> 'I think it's worth considering now, because of the changing roles and because of the number of demands, whether what we had in the past – a generic job description – is what's needed in the future, or whether you should be looking to have wider multi-disciplinary teams, where you have people who are particularly experienced and qualified in family work as opposed to advocacy or social work, health professionals – all sorts of different experiences.'

There were plans at Leeds Safe House, before its closure, to develop a more multi-disciplinary team. This may be necessary for any project which aims to work flexibly and responsively.

Safety of staff

To some extent, it is an inevitable feature of working with young people who run away that staff will sometimes find themselves in risky situations. However, it is clearly essential to attempt to minimise these risks, and projects have developed a range of good-practice principles in order to achieve this goal.

Before considering some of these principles it is worth exploring the nature of the risks faced by staff, partly in an effort to challenge some natural preconceptions. Perhaps the most obvious risk that springs to mind is for detached workers on the streets of a city centre. Yet, in fact, serious assaults on staff in these situations have been extremely rare at Youth Link and Safe in the City. This may have been partly due to the precautions taken by the projects, but there are also aspects of these situations which might make them less risky than would first appear:

> *'There clearly are risks but it would be easy to sensationalise these, because it is easy to perceive it as a dangerous activity. Some of the risks are no more or less than you would face as an individual or a couple in the middle of Manchester on a Friday night when people are coming out of the clubs and pubs. You are facing the same risk of violence, street robbery and aggression.'*

The following list provides some of the key aspects of maximising worker safety while on the streets, based on the practice of Safe in the City and Youth Link:
- workers always work in pairs, never split up, maintain easy eye contact at all times
- workers always have access to a mobile phone
- workers always have access to a manager via telephone (including a designated manager on duty outside office hours)
- there is an agreement that if one worker is uncomfortable with doing something, it's not done, and that there is no discussion about this at the time
- workers agree a code with which to communicate in difficult situations
- the project provides clear information about areas where staff should be extra-vigilant and areas which they should not visit
- time is allotted at the start of the session for discussion between the pair of workers about strengths and weaknesses
- staff work in mixed-gender pairs when practical.

There clearly arc also risks attached to doing other forms of work with young people who run away. In terms of refuge work, there are risks to staff within the accommodation provision, and also in travelling to meet young people at unknown destinations in the middle of the night. Contributors from Leeds Safe House and the Porth Project commented on their concern, in retrospect, about the way in which the project met young people. At Leeds, one worker went out alone in the project car, with a mobile phone, and stayed in regular contact with the refuge. However, at night, when there were only two workers on duty and one senior member of staff on call, this could leave both workers in a vulnerable position. At Porth, two workers went out to meet young people. However, due to the size of the staff team, for several years there was no additional on-call safety net out of office hours. This is an issue which needs to be seriously considered in any future provision of confidential refuge as there are huge resource implications in ensuring pair working at all times.

There are also risks for workers at missing persons schemes visiting young people and families, which have also been addressed by the provision of mobile phones and a system of reporting back to the project base (or an out-of-hours contact) when the visit is completed.

Stresses on staff

Apart from safety issues, there are a range of emotional and physical stresses on staff working in projects with young people who run away. Perhaps the most significant of these stresses is the emotional impact of hearing young people's stories, and often a feeling of powerless to change things for individual young people. The young-person-centred approach and tight confidentiality policy both exacerbate these stresses. It is not uncommon for workers to have to end contact with a young person knowing that they are going to return to a potentially harmful situation:

> *'What you see and hear can be quite traumatic. And you do sort of think, "God, I wish I could put a stop to this", but I think that as workers you go in with your eyes open and say, "This is what's happening and I'm not here to rescue these young people. I can't measure success on a young person coming out of what's happening now, I have to measure success on where I'm at with each individual young person."'*

On top of this, there is the frustration and anger that workers feel when they have done substantial work with a young person which has ultimately failed to achieve any sort of satisfactory outcome:

> *'Some situations have left us furious, angry and fed up, and on the edge of burn-out about certain situations where we haven't been able to get the desired outcome. For a lot of workers that is their own burn-out because you often don't know the outcomes of your work, you don't have something you can measure at the end of the year.'*

There are also more practical stresses involved in many of the projects, including working anti-social hours on disruptive rota patterns, or spending time out on the streets in winter.

Supervision and support

Given the range of stresses that workers face and the complexity of some of the work being undertaken by the projects, good structures for supervision and support are vital to the successful maintenance of a staff team, and of good-quality practice. The projects have approached these support needs in differing ways, partly to fit particular models of working. There is emphasis on, and commitment to, regular line-management supervision for workers, but it is clear that there are a range of needs requiring a range of different types of support.

In street-work projects there is always an opportunity for staff to debrief after the session, with someone who did not participate in the street-work session. If the session ended outside office hours, this role is filled by an on-call manager over the telephone. Both street-work projects place a high priority on debriefing, including regular opportunities for the staff team to do this as a group:

> *'We ask workers often to go home who've walked away from situations because they've made an assessment that, at that moment in time, that young person out on the streets is safer than where we might want them to be – and that's incredibly stressful, so you build in things like supervision, practice meetings, to enable that dialogue. An unsafe place would be where people don't feel able to say, "I'm really struggling with this, I stayed awake last night."'*

One of the missing persons projects has a contract with a mental health team to provide regular confidential individual consultancy to workers, which gives them an opportunity to talk through the feelings raised by the work outside the staff team. Other projects were aiming to develop similar support systems, and this was seen as an important part of maintaining a high standard of professional practice in this field of work:

> *'Some information you get can bring up a lot of other things for you. I want to feel very clear in my responses to young people, I don't want them to feel rejected, I want to be open, I want to feel like I've done the best job I can, and often in ordinary supervision there isn't time to look at the detailed interactions, but I think that is very important.'*

Aside from the concrete aspects of support structures, some contributors emphasised the need for the right environment within the staff team to enable people to ask for and be provided with support. There is a need to create a culture which tolerates mistakes, accepts vulnerability and values honesty. One contributor argued that there was a need to counteract a macho approach to working with this target group:

> *'Street work and detached work often comes with a very macho image of being tough, being out on the streets at the cutting edge, and you have to keep balancing that with [the fact that] if you're not willing to feel vulnerable at times within this environment, you may make decisions that have implications for young people or yourself really.'*

The induction of new staff can also be a particularly important area in projects working with young people who run away:

> *'The work with young people on the streets can make demands on staff that far exceed what they may have experienced before... The adjustment to working in that kind of way can be quite difficult for staff that haven't come from a street-work background, so we have a very considered induction.'*

Management issues

So far this chapter has focused on the issues relating to practice staff in projects. Given the above discussion, it is also clear that there are a range of challenges facing managers of staff in projects working with young people who run away.

The unpredictability of the work was one key issue identified:

> *'You walked through the door and you could never go in with an agenda that "I'm going to do this, this and this" because two or three things would hit you immediately when you walked in which you hadn't planned for.'*

Senior practitioners and project managers are expected to offer on-call telephone support out of hours, usually on a rota basis, at most of the projects discussed in this report. Usually this support facility is used regularly or intermittently by project workers, either to 'offload' about the impact of the work, or to discuss difficult decisions, such as those relating to breaches of confidentiality and child protection issues. This has a particularly marked effect on managers in 24-hour accommodation projects, with a feeling of the work always being present, and difficulty in shutting off from it:

> *'You don't switch off at all; even when you're not on call it's still a 24-hour machine that goes on when you're not there... I found that extremely demanding, extremely draining.'*

There is a very high degree of responsibility placed on managers in terms of making decisions about sensitive issues in situations which often require a rapid response.

It seems also to be common for managers to face a high level of challenge from project staff in many of the projects. One contributor felt that this was intrinsic to the work, given the emphasis on recruiting staff with strong advocacy skills and the willingness to work independently in difficult situations:

'I think, because of the nature of the job, the people that get attracted to it are usually very clear in their expectations and I think that managing a team of that nature can be more demanding than managing a youth club setting... It's probably to do with the fact that we spend a lot of our time advocating for young people and therefore we're quite happy to advocate on behalf of ourselves... As a manager you have to be prepared to listen to people and hear their views and accept that sometimes you have to make adjustments [because of] what people are feeling. There needs to be flexibility in the management to do that.'

However, at times, the level of challenge seems to have become a heavy burden for managers at some projects:

'Managers would apparently be responsible for everything and have all those pressures on them, and the workers would expect management in that sense to take ultimate responsibility, but at the same time felt totally free to undermine and abuse all management activity.'

Finally, the stresses on workers discussed earlier can spill over into a high demand for support from managers:

'Because your client group is extremely needy and vulnerable, I think those patterns are replicated in the worker groups, so the teams are needy as well – they're dealing with needy people and they become very needy and depleted themselves, and so they turn to a limited number of managers for all kinds of support, overt and covert.'

All in all, management posts in projects working with young people who run away are likely to be highly demanding and stressful, and an awareness of this should be built into recruitment procedures and into the support and supervision structures that are put in place for these posts.

Key points

- In recruiting practitioners and managers for projects working with young people who run away, a balance needs to be struck within the team between skills in engaging with detached young people and the skills needed to work on issues such as child protection in conjunction with other agencies.

- If projects are to provide a range of services to meet young people's diverse needs, there may be a case for the creation of multi-disciplinary teams with specialist posts for different styles of work such as advocacy and family mediation.

- Careful thought needs to be given to policies, practices and procedures that can maximise staff safety, particularly for refuge and street-work projects.

- Work with young people who run away is often emotionally draining for staff. High-quality supervision is vital and there is also a need for the creation of a mutually supportive environment where staff can talk openly about their feelings regarding the work. There is also a case for external individual consultancy to be made available to staff.

- The management of projects for young runaways is a difficult and challenging task. The work is extremely unpredictable and a high degree of responsibility is placed on senior practitioners and managers in terms of decision-making, often including being instantly available out-of-office hours. The impact of the work on practitioners may also have knock-on effects on line managers who may face a high degree of challenge from the staff team.

12

Developmental issues

This final chapter on contributors' views picks up on comments which have not been covered so far, and which can be broadly termed 'developmental issues'. These include ways of publicising services, resource issues, issues relating to developing services within a wider organisational context, young people's participation, and learning related to the conduct of research and evaluation with young people who run away.

Publicity

Research has revealed that many young people who run away have had no previous contact with helping agencies and are unaware of services in their area that might be of assistance to them. Clearly, then, the effective publicising of services is a major priority and challenge for projects working with this target group.

It seems that traditional forms of publicity, such as posters and leaflets, are not particularly effective. Several contributors emphasised the need for face-to-face contact with young people, in order to give an impression of what the project was like. A number of projects have done a series of presentations at local schools, and at Checkpoint and the Porth Project this has been followed by a significant upturn in referrals from young people under 16. This therefore seems a useful strategy, but it is resource-intensive and needs to be repeated annually.

Indirect approaches also seem to have had some success. Youth Link and the Porth Project noticed increases in referrals following efforts to publicise their service through other local agencies. However, this is obviously only going to reach young people who already use other services.

Ultimately, for most projects, the major source of publicity has been word-of-mouth recommendation by other young people. Initial contacts with young people, even relatively minor ones such as one minute spent with a young person on the streets, can therefore be important in promoting a service. Clearly, this form of publicity will take a long time to build up.

Resource issues

A number of contributors commented on the resource-intensive nature of work with young people who run away, and the need to be realistic about what can be achieved with a finite amount of resources. Some details of costs of refuge projects were provided in Chapter 3. Leeds Safe House cost around £500,000 a year. Porth Project had a budget of £350,000 but often struggled to maintain a service and was, in the view of staff there, significantly under-resourced. In both these projects the large majority of resources went into staff costs.

Street-work projects also are fairly labour-intensive. For example, the annual budget of Youth Link's street work/drop-in service is around £180,000. This includes around eight street-work sessions a week, plus the maintenance of the drop-in centre on weekdays. If a street-work model is chosen, a certain minimum amount of work must be done each week, otherwise the familiarity and credibility of the project on the streets will be difficult to establish:

> 'Like any level of service, you have to be doing enough of it [so] that people know it exists and can make contact with it – doing one session a fortnight is pointless. You cannot build up the relationships with the street agencies and the street community and get linked into that intelligence grapevine and have a physical presence there. You really need to do, I think, four to five sessions a week over a spread of times and days, otherwise you might as well not bother; you're better off using other methods, and those other methods are less expensive to resource.'

Missing persons schemes and centre-based projects appear to be the cheapest options, particularly if they are integrated into a wider service network as in Checkpoint. The South Coast Runaways Initiative runs on just one full-time post plus some sessional staffing, together with a contribution to the costs of running the centre.

Whichever model of work is chosen (with the possible exception of a daytime centre-based model), consideration must be given to out-of-hours and on-call payments. This has been a difficult issue at some projects, particularly where staff are expected to be available via telephone for lengthy periods outside office hours on the basis of a small lump-sum payment. At times it seems that some projects have been able to maintain an out-of-hours service only thanks to high levels of commitment and goodwill of staff, but these conditions may not be easily replicable on a wider basis.

The benefits of integrating services in terms of efficient use of resources were noted by several contributors. For example, Youth Link is able to provide a responsive service to young people through a range of referral routes, due to the size of the staff team. The demand for services via the missing persons scheme has been sporadic, but it has been possible to absorb this demand within a daily pool of resources also catering for drop-in and street work. If such a scheme had been set up independently, the variation in demand might have meant a significant amount of wasted resources.

Organisational issues

With the exception of the ASTRA Project, all the projects contributing to this study are part of a larger organisation. At times this has created difficulties for projects in relation to organisational policies and also to young people's views.

A particular area for tension is that of confidentiality and child protection policies. Large organisations will tend to have standard policies on these issues which are applicable to a range of projects working in different ways with a diverse range of children, young people and families. The relatively unusual approach taken by projects working with young people who run away will often conflict with these policies. There is therefore a need for some flexibility in organisational policy, without which projects are unlikely to be successful in engaging effectively with young people in the target group. Organisations involved in this area of work need to be aware of this issue and of the inherent risk-taking approach that is necessary. It has usually proved possible for projects to develop appropriate policies within the context of a large organisation, but this does require a high degree of commitment and support for the approach on the part of senior managers:

> 'We have a lot of projects coming along asking whether they can use our confidentiality policy "off the shelf". We say, "Great! However, if you end up in court or another environment where you have to explain it, do you own it, do you understand where you fit in to the law, do you know what that means for you as an individual?"'

The inherently risky nature of work with young people who run away can also have other kinds of implications for organisations. The Children's Society has successfully managed to maintain a programme of work in this field for over two decades, and this has necessitated making changes within the organisation (for example, a review of foster-caring policy) and on campaigning for changes in the external environment. The organisation has at times taken significant risks, such as setting up refuges when there was no legal framework. It has also campaigned on some difficult areas, such as changes in the way young people who are involved in the sex industry are treated in law. There can be a tension between tackling social injustices and the need for voluntary organisations to maintain a particular image and bring in funding. These tensions seem to be particularly likely to emerge in this field and an organisation needs to be prepared for this if it embarks on work with young people who run away.

Young people's participation

There is growing recognition within the field of social welfare work of the importance of involving service users in the development and running of services. This is quite a challenge for any project, but there are particular issues in working with young people who run away which make this task more difficult. The young people with whom the projects work often have particularly chaotic lives and efforts to involve them in project development have sometimes foundered because of this.

Given the nature of many of the young people's lives, it is important also to view participation as a matter of choice on their part. Young people in crisis will often have more pressing priorities than participating in project development, and neither may they wish to be contacted once the work is over:

> 'Primarily the young people in these sorts of situations are wanting to sort out their crisis rather than comment on service delivery! They want to know how to comment on it if it's bad practice, but that's not their first and foremost thought.'

Leeds Safe House attempted on several occasions to have consultation days with young people who had used the project but, despite considerable efforts, attendance was very low. There have been some successes in this respect. Safe in the City recently involved young people in the recruitment process for staff, which required a consistent level of commitment, including preparation days. However, it was noted by one contributor that this was achieved through working with young people who had had contact with the project but had returned to a semi-stable situation. The Children's Society has also, on several occasions, involved young people in the dissemination of research findings, including doing interviews with the media. A point of learning from both the above initiatives has been the importance of keeping issues of support and confidentiality at the forefront at all times. Any engagement with young people who run away can raise unanticipated issues, and clarity over the boundaries of confidentiality, and a commitment to provide the ongoing support to young people after the concrete task has been completed are vital elements of good practice.

A point made by several contributors was the need to devise modes of participation that are relevant to the way young people live their lives, rather than expecting young people to fit into adult professional ways of working, such as steering groups. In general, more immediate spontaneous forms of feedback and gathering views have proved to be more effective than highly-structured ones. Leeds Safe House devised a questionnaire, which was used for several years and proved to be a valuable way of gathering immediate feedback from a wide range of young people using the service. Questionnaires can be very popular with young people if well designed. Safe in the City has a computer for young people with tailor-made software designed to gather feedback in a fairly unstructured way.

Finally, it was noted by several contributors that a commitment to participation will have to be matched by a significant commitment of resources. It is easy to lose sight of long-term goals when the issues raised by day-to-day work are so pressing:

> *'The lessons learned... are, if you don't plan for it it won't happen, if you don't put resources into it it won't happen, and even if you do plan for it and put resources in, it can still be difficult.'*

It may therefore be necessary to allot dedicated staff resources in order to pursue a consistent development of young people's participation within a project, particularly when the nature of the practice work is unpredictable and crisis-oriented.

Research and evaluation

Research findings have made a significant contribution to the development of models of practice in this field of work. There is now a body of knowledge at a general level which can be of use in planning work with this target group. (A summary of research-based knowledge can be found in Chapter 2.) Nevertheless, it has been suggested elsewhere in the report that there may often be a need for small-scale research projects as a prelude to project development, in order to learn about local needs or the issues affecting particular target groups. In view of this, a brief overview of learning points from previous research with young people who run away is provided in this section.

In terms of methodology, three particular difficulties have been encountered in attempting to do research into this target group.

First, it is no easy task to draw up clear definitions of the phenomenon being studied. Some of the early research studies focused on reported incidence of running away to the police, but is has become apparent that this has a fairly weak association with actual rates of running away, and it seems inadvisable to conduct a research study on the basis of this definition. General surveys of young people have tended to rely on self-definition of 'running away' or 'being forced to leave' and this has proved to be a relatively successful strategy, provided sufficient information is gathered about the incident to be able to root out any misunderstandings. In terms of interviewing young people, definitions can be explored with young people face-to-face but it can be difficult to identify appropriate young people in the first place. Studies which rely on professionals to identify relevant young people need to build in some checks because professionals often confuse the issue of running away with that of youth homelessness.

Second, it has not been easy to obtain for research purposes good samples of young people who run away. Studies have been most successful when they have been spontaneous in making contact with young people, but even so, there have been difficulties. The 'Running – the Risk' study (Stein, Rees and Frost, 1994) had resources equivalent to the cost of a full-time researcher plus management and other expenses for a two-year period. It has also had the commitment of an organisation and direct links into four projects working with young people who run away. Yet interviews were obtained with only 28 young people. More recently, the 'Still Running' research (Safe on the Streets Research Team, 1999) was successful in interviewing over 200 young people, most of whom had experience of running away under the age of 16, but this project had a substantial investment of resources. Even in large samples it is difficult to ensure that specific sub-groups are well represented, and particular thought needs to be given to strategies which will adequately reach young people from minority groups (including on the basis of ethnicity, sexuality and disability).

A third methodological issue is the difficulty of carrying out follow-up studies. Several attempts to do this (e.g., Stein, Rees and Frost, 1994) have met with only limited success. The nature of the lives of young people who run away, in terms of mobility and disruption, make follow-up studies particularly problematic. They are likely to require a large investment of resources for a relatively small return.

Apart from these methodological issues, prospective researchers in this field should be aware of the need for particularly well-developed research policies and practice standards, due to the sensitive nature of the research topic. Research experience has shown that participants can often make fresh disclosures of abuse and other events during interviews, so there is as much need for clarity regarding confidentiality and child protection policies in research as when undertaking practice-based work. Essentially, researchers should ensure that there is a full explanation of these policies before the interview begins, and adequate time given for debriefing at the end of the interview. There has also been a significant level of disclosure through self-completed questionnaires, so it is vital to decide whether these are to be anonymous and, if not, how issues of concern are to be followed up and dealt with.

In face-to-face research contact with young people who run away it is also vital to be clear about roles and boundaries. If the interview is a strictly one-off encounter, then young people should be aware of this and researchers should be prepared with local information about relevant services so that if young people raise issues that may need to be followed up, they can be referred to these services as appropriate.

Finally, as with practice-based work with this target group, the emotional impact on researchers should not be under-estimated. It has proved necessary to provide significant levels of support and debriefing to interviewers and office-based researchers analysing data, and the resources and structures for this should be built into the design of the project.

All in all, research into this area raises up a range of difficult issues and organisations undertaking such research need to be well prepared and appropriately skilled in dealing with these issues.

Key points

- Efforts to publicise projects for young runaways amongst young people have met with mixed success, and it seems that the main source of publicity is word-of-mouth recommendation by other young people.

- There are large differences in costs of the different models so far utilised in the UK. Refuge projects have been the most expensive, but street-work projects also require a substantial investment. Missing persons' schemes and initiatives integrated into centre-based services are less expensive options.

- Where a runaway project is run by a large organisation, the tailor-made policies and practice needed to work effectively with young runaways will require a high degree of flexibility and a certain amount of risk-taking on the part of the organisation, if the initiatives are to be successful.

- Projects attempting to involve young people actively in their development have often encountered difficulties in view of the nature of young runaways' lives and the issues they face. The successful achievement of participation of young people in this target group is likely to require dedicated resources and an ongoing commitment on the part of projects.

- People considering embarking on research with young runaways should be aware of the range of methodological difficulties which have been encountered in this field, and the need to prepare thorough approaches to ethical issues such as confidentiality and the handling of disclosures of information by young people.

13

CONCLUSIONS

Introduction

This final chapter draws together some of the key themes and debates discussed throughout the report, with the aim of providing a summary of the key issues to be considered in developing and managing initiatives which work with young runaways. Inevitably, the choice of a manageable list of key points will be selective and some detail will be lost. Readers are, therefore, also referred to the summaries of key points at the end of each chapter for a more complete overview of the issues covered in the report.

The key issues presented in this chapter are divided into five broad areas:

1. Issues to be considered in making decisions about the kinds of services to develop

2. Issues to be considered in making decisions about methods of engaging and working with young runaways and their families

3. Issues to be considered in the early developmental stages of initiatives

4. Issues to be considered in planning the ongoing management of initiatives

5. Issues to be considered in terms of placing work with young runaways into a broader context.

Developing practice models to work with runaways

This section summarises the key issues to be considered when making decisions about what kinds of services are to be developed to work with young people who run away. The focus here is on making decisions about specific practice models. Many of the points made in the report also point to the need for more integrated models of working with this target group. This issue is discussed in the final section of the chapter.

Matching the model to the intended target group

Research indicates that around one in nine young people run away overnight before the age of 16. Inevitably there is a large amount of diversity within this category of young people. The discussion in Chapters 3 to 7 illustrates that the main practice models developed so far in the UK have each been successful in engaging with different sub-groups within the overall population of young runaways. For example, a city-centre-based street-work model is particularly effective in engaging with very marginalised and detached young people who have usually run away many times, but is not effective in engaging with first-time runaways. It is therefore vital to be clear about the intended target group of an initiative and to be aware of the implications of choosing a particular model of service delivery.

It is important also to note that the existing models have not been equally successful in engaging effectively with all young runaways. Contributors expressed concerns about the ability of the current models to work with young people from minority groups (on the basis of ethnicity, sexuality or ability) as discussed in Chapter 10. There has also been a tendency to focus on older runaways and, so far, a relatively small level of engagement with the under-11 age group. As pointed out in Chapter 2, this is a particularly significant group of runaways as there is a tendency for young people who start running away before the age of 11 to go on to run away repeatedly as teenagers.

Fitting the model to the local context

A second key issue relates to finding a match between the kind of model developed and the local context. There is a need, as discussed later, to gather local information on which to base decisions about service development. The report has provided a number of examples of services which have been found to work well within a particular local context, such as the ASTRA Project (see Chapter 5) and the South Coast Runaways Initiative (see Chapter 6). These services would not necessarily work well if transplanted to another local area, and with this target group it seems vital to take local contextual issues into account when planning the development of services.

It is notable that, to date, there has been virtually no service development for young runaways in rural areas. However, research indicates that running away rates are just as high in rural as in urban areas. There is therefore a major challenge here if a range of services is to be developed which meet the needs of all young people who run away in the UK.

Whether to offer emergency accommodation

When developing initiatives to work with young people who have run away, the decision whether to offer short-term emergency accommodation is key. There was a shared view amongst contributors that whilst most young runaways do not necessarily need or want temporary accommodation, a significant minority do have such a need. Most of the projects described in this report do not provide accommodation, but managers and practitioners have often experienced this as a shortcoming when working with young people in particularly vulnerable situations (see Chapters 5 and 6 for further discussion). On the other hand, in the view of some contributors, there are drawbacks to offering accommodation in terms of gaining a speedy resolution to young people's problems, and this seems to be particularly salient in relation to working with very detached young people in street work situations.

Resource implications of different models

Decisions about models of service delivery also need to be tied in with resource considerations. The main models discussed in Chapters 3 to 7 vary widely in terms of costs. Models including an emergency accommodation element tend to be relatively costly, and there are also significant costs involved in running an adequate street-work model. Centre-based models which 'add on' to existing services and missing person schemes tend to be cheaper models. See Chapter 12 for further discussion of this issue.

Issues of engaging with young runaways

Whichever practice model is chosen, the report has highlighted some key issues that are likely to be faced in developing ways of working with young runaways.

Methods of contacting young people

There is a key decision to be made about the extent to which any service is 'self-commissioned' by the young person. Most of the projects contributing to this report have tended to adopt an approach which emphasises the young person's choice in whether to take up services. This approach has generally been successful. However, this does not preclude projects being active in initially making contact with young people in the target group. For example, the street-work projects initiate contact with young people on the streets, and the ASTRA Project makes great efforts to contact young people directly and quickly (see Chapter 5). Whilst all the projects have accepted referrals from other agencies, this has usually been on the basis of also having a discussion with the young person at the point of referral to ensure that the referral is something the young person wants. In order to ensure that services are accessible to all young people who run away, contributors have emphasised the need for a range of means for young people to make contact, including drop-in facilities, a free telephone line and e-mail contact.

Balancing a young-person-centred approach with engaging with families

The existing models of intervention with young people running away from the family home have tended to be highly focused on the young person as an individual, rather than on the family. There are some good reasons for this focus, particularly the need to establish a relationship with the young person, which has been a key success of all of the projects discussed in this report. However, this approach, if taken too far, does have the drawback that it fails to engage with the key reasons for running away which are linked to relationships within the family home. There is a need therefore to pilot and develop approaches which retain the ability to engage with young people but also allow the possibility of family-based interventions. The solution-focused brief therapy model used by the Home & Away Project is one possibility, but there is also scope to test out other approaches, such as family mediation and family group conferencing.

Methods of working with young people and families

Along with the young-person-centred approach there has been a tendency for many of the projects working with young runaways to adopt an advocacy model of working with young people. The advantages and disadvantages of this model are reviewed in Chapter 8. There was a commonly-held view amongst contributors that whilst advocacy was an appropriate way of working with some young people in certain situations, its use had been too extensive. There is a need to pilot and refine other approaches which place more emphasis on working with young people and other family members. These might include the models of family interventions mentioned above. Ultimately it may be desirable for projects working with young runaways to offer a range of approaches which can fit different situations, rather than be limited to the employment of one pre-determined approach.

Catering for young people's longer-term needs

A key issue facing all projects working with young people who run away relates to the handling of the long-term needs of some young people. The projects have tended to adopt short-term crisis intervention models, which focus on speedy resolutions to the problems that caused young people to run away from home. For some young people this may be an adequate response, but for others, particularly those for whom the problems they are facing are of a long-standing nature, crisis intervention alone is not sufficient. Projects report difficulties in referring these young people to other services which may be able to cater for these longer-term needs, and there is therefore a possibility of repetitive crisis intervention work with some young people. This is a key issue for the further development of integrated and comprehensive responses to the needs of young people who run away.

The development and setting up of projects and initiatives

The need for local information

As indicated in an earlier section, whilst research suggests that there is a similar level of running away in all types of geographical areas, there may still be significant variations in the options open to young people who run away within specific areas, and a variation in links with other issues that are important in those areas. It is therefore desirable to gather local information about the incidence of running away, the experiences of young people who have run away within the area and the current services which are available to young people who run away or are at risk of running away.

The need to engage key local agencies

The need to engage local agencies in planned work with young runaways has been emphasised at various points in the report. Young people who run away tend also to have a range of other issues in their lives, as discussed in the research summary in Chapter 2. Any initiative working with this target group will therefore inevitably need to have working contacts with a range of agencies, including the police, social services, education, and health and local voluntary agencies working with young people and families.

The need to engage in a dialogue with key local agencies was perhaps the point most commonly emphasised by contributors. Projects which had effectively carried out this task had often been dogged by difficulties with inter-agency relationships in their early years. One aspect of engaging with other agencies at the developmental stage is the value of developing protocols with other agencies which clarify roles, policies, expectations, and so on.

The development of policies

Contributors highlighted the need to develop good policies to deal with several issues which are particularly important when working with young people who have run away. Among these, perhaps the most significant are policies in relation to confidentiality and child protection (see Chapter 8 for further discussion), and clear guidelines and working practices which promote staff safety (see Chapter 11).

Decisions about recruitment and structuring of the staff team

Based on the experiences of contributing projects, decisions made about the skills of staff and the structure of the staff team tend to have far-reaching implications. One important issue relates to the kinds of skills and experience which staff should have. Practitioners working with young runaways need to have a range of skills, including the ability to engage quickly and effectively with marginalised young people as well as the ability to deal effectively with, for example, child protection issues. Many contributors felt that it was important to have a range of backgrounds among the staff team, including some practitioners or managers with statutory social services qualifications and experience and some with a more youth-work oriented background. A second issue relates to the multi-disciplinary nature of working with young runaways. Contributors at some of the larger projects felt that it might be helpful to move away from generic job descriptions and develop a staff team with a range of specialisms (e.g., advocacy workers, family mediation workers) to deal with young people in different situations.

Potentially long developmental periods

A final point to be borne in mind when planning the setting-up of services for young runaways is the length of time which has been required before some projects have begun to work with young people. This issue seems to be particularly significant for projects providing emergency accommodation where the need to gain the approval of key local agencies and meet a range of legal requirements has led to much longer development times than was anticipated. Typically, projects of this kind have experienced a gap of between 12 and 24 months between the employment of the first member of staff and the start of work with young people. It seems important therefore for people initiating projects to be aware of, and plan for, a potentially long developmental period.

The ongoing management of initiatives

Training, supervision and support of staff

The challenges facing managers of projects were emphasised in Chapter 11. Working in a young-person-centred way with young people who run away places considerable stress on practitioners. The effective supervision and support for practitioners to ensure their welfare and safe practice will be a major aspect of the job of managers of projects working with young runaways. In addition, senior practitioners and managers face extra stresses due to the unpredictable nature of the work, the need to make key decisions on the spur of the moment, often outside normal office hours, and the challenges that they may face from staff.

Key issues to be considered in terms of developing the skills base of the staff team are training in dealing with child protection issues for all staff members (this would include administrative and other staff who would not necessarily have skills in this area) and the need to develop the cultural competence of the staff team (see the

Appendix) so that services are accessible and responsive to the needs of young people from a diverse range of backgrounds.

Management of child protection issues

There was almost unanimous agreement amongst contributors that an appropriate confidentiality policy was one of the most vital foundations of effective engagement with young people who run away. The projects have generally adopted a higher threshold of confidentiality than the majority of social welfare agencies working with children and young people. Contributors have emphasised the high burden of responsibility that this places on managers and practitioners, both in terms of developing exemplary models of practice and in terms of decision-making about individual cases. Projects have developed sophisticated means of trying to ensure that their practice in terms of confidentiality and child protection is to a high standard. The approaches adopted have been endorsed by recent government guidance, and also by local ACPCs and social services departments.

This issue is a key area for anyone involved in developing, managing or undertaking practice-based work with young people who run away. Practice experience and research findings indicate that these young people often experience high levels of abuse, neglect and mistreatment on an ongoing basis. The appropriate balance in addressing these issues effectively whilst maintaining young people's trust is absolutely vital to successful and professional work with this target group.

Maintenance of external relationships

The barriers to good working relationships with other agencies presented by the young-person-centred approach have been extensively covered in Chapters 8 and 9 of this report. The adoption of an 'advocacy' approach and of a high threshold of confidentiality are both factors which create inherent tensions in working in partnership with other agencies. The early experiences of projects working with young people who run away clearly illustrate the potential for conflict due to the above tensions. However, over recent years there have been improvements in the quality of relationships between most of the projects and the local agencies with whom they work. This may be partly due to a change in professional attitudes to young people's rights and participation, but it appears to have been primarily due to a more realistic and refined approach on the part of projects working with young people who run away.

This improvement is encouraging but it is inevitable that tensions will remain between primarily voluntary sector projects working with young runaways who are in urgent need of a range of services, and statutory sector agencies working within a tight set of resource and policy constraints. Thus, contributors have emphasised the need for continued dialogue, sharing of information and expertise, realistic expectations and co-operative working wherever possible in order to minimise the impact of these tensions on the day-to-day individual work with young people.

Participation of young people

The projects contributing to this report have often made considerable effort to involve young people in the review and development of project work. Whilst there have been some successes, projects have also encountered a considerable amount of difficulty in this respect. The chaotic nature of the lives of many young runaways, and the short-term or sporadic nature of project interventions, have tended to make it difficult to gain a high level of participation amongst young people who use projects. If there is to be more success in this respect in the future, there is a need to plan for participation and to develop methods of participation which fit in with the realities of the lives of young runaways (see Chapter 12).

Broader issues

Preventative work

Social welfare initiatives are often viewed as being placed on a continuum of primary, secondary and tertiary interventions. Viewing the history of work with young runaways in the UK on this basis, there was initially a concentration of models at the tertiary level (e.g., street work and refuge), focusing primarily on young people who have already run away a number of times or who are living on the streets. More recently there has been greater emphasis on secondary interventions targeted at young people in the early stages of running away, through the development of missing person schemes and centre-based work. However, relatively little has been done in terms of primary intervention which aims to prevent running away occurring in the first place. There are a few isolated examples such as the peer counselling scheme in Leeds and the Internet service at Youth Link, but these models are still being developed. The concept of preventing running away is a major challenge as there are no reliable diagnostic instruments to identify potential runaways (and it is highly unlikely that it is possible to develop such instruments, given the diversity of the phenomenon). However, there is scope to pilot approaches modelled in other countries such as educational initiatives, including peer education (see the Appendix). There is also a need to integrate the issue of running away into other preventative and awareness-raising initiatives, such as those focusing on youth homelessness.

The need for integrated models

It is clear from the preceding discussion that no single model will effectively meet the needs of young people who run away. There is a large amount of diversity within this group of young people and this needs to be reflected in a diverse range of services. A comprehensive network of services for young people who run away would include elements of all the four major models outlined in Chapters 3 to 6. An integrated and inclusive practice model would have three key characteristics.

First it would need to offer young people a variety of means of getting in touch, as discussed earlier in this chapter. This would include the possibility of self-referral (either face-to-face or over the telephone), referral by other agencies or concerned people, and various forms of outreach work.

Second, once contact is made there needs to be a range of services available to meet the diverse and complex needs of young people who run away. These services would need to be flexible in location (e.g., working in a centre, on the streets, or in the young person's home) and in approach including practical support, information, counselling, advocacy and family-focused work.

Third, an integrated model of service provision would need to have an emergency accommodation element for some young people. It is clear from contributors' experiences and comments that there is a significant minority of young runaways who are in need of a safe place to stay for a short while, and that this is a prerequisite to undertaking successful work with them.

The US models described in the Appendix offer a blueprint for the kinds of integrated services which may be needed to provide a comprehensive response to the needs of young people who run away within any given local area. It may be possible to develop such networks of services in large population centres, perhaps through partnerships between a consortium of statutory and voluntary organisations.

For more sparsely populated areas, this kind of dedicated model of services for runaways may not be sustainable, and it will, perhaps, be necessary to explore the potential for integrating services for runaways into existing voluntary and statutory provision for young people, as some projects described within the report have begun to attempt. Efforts to reach out to young people can be undertaken in partnership with existing community-based agencies, an approach which is currently being piloted by Safe in the City in Manchester to work with black young people. Centre-based models of service provision can be located within existing centres for young people, as illustrated by the South Coast Runaways Initiative and the Breaking Free Project. Models of emergency accommodation do not need to follow the centralised refuge approach (although this may be a cost-effective model in large cities) but could be developed as flexible add-on to existing services as currently operated by the Home & Away Project.

There are therefore clearly possibilities for integrating work with runaways into existing service provision for children and young people through the employment of specialist workers with the skills and expertise to work with this target group. However, the extent to which such integration is possible will depend on the ability of existing services to accommodate the kinds of philosophy, policies, practices and structures which have been developed in order to successfully work with this target group.

The need to embed the issue of running away within existing structures

Much of the work carried out with young people who run away in the UK has been undertaken by voluntary organisations and has often taken place partly or wholly outside larger frameworks and structures underpinning work with children and young people. Whilst this has offered the opportunity to develop innovative practice models, it has also limited the extent to which running away has been taken on as a core issue affecting young people. In order to provide a comprehensive response to the needs of young runaways, it may be necessary to embed the issue of running away into current structures, frameworks and agendas, such as Connections in England and Social Inclusion Partnerships in Scotland.

Research has indicated that running away has strong links with a number of other problematic issues in young people's lives and that it is associated with a process of social exclusion for some young people. It can therefore be argued that an effective response to running away is a key component of the social inclusion agenda and that it should be incorporated into national and local frameworks and initiatives which aim to tackle social exclusion.

Concluding comments

This report has provided an overview of a significant programme of work which, through practice and research, has explored the needs of a vulnerable group of young people and has gradually developed and refined ways of working with these young people which offer them help with the problems they are facing. The work so far carried out with young runaways in the UK provides evidence of the ability of social welfare organisations to identify and tackle key issues of social justice and produce significant and positive change.

Despite the considerable successes so far achieved in this field of work, significant challenges still remain before there can be said to be a comprehensive response to the needs of young people who run away or are at risk of running away. There are still many gaps and under-explored areas of working with this target group and minority populations whose particular needs and issues have not been fully explored or addressed. At a more general level, there is a need for work with runaways to be brought into the mainstream and to be embedded within existing structures and frameworks which aim to meet the needs of disadvantaged children and young people. Given the evidence on the nature of the problems faced by young people who run away, this task is an important aspect of promoting the social inclusion of all children and young people.

Appendix: Alternative approaches in other countries

Introduction

The main focus of this publication is on learning from projects in the UK which have worked specifically with young people who run away, over the past two decades. However, young runaways and street children are a global phenomenon, and in view of this it is relevant to look at models that have been developed in other countries to work with these young people.

Most of the material for this chapter has been gathered via the Internet. This is inevitably a 'hit and miss' affair, and no claims are made for the completeness of the information presented here. There are literally hundreds of projects (mostly in the USA) and a comprehensive guide to these would constitute a substantial document in its own right. This appendix has the more modest goal of describing ways of working with young runaways which have been utilised in other countries but have not so far been tried in the UK, with the intention of bringing alternative approaches to the attention of those who may be considering developing new initiatives.

Inevitably the nature of this phenomenon varies hugely according to cultural contexts. Many 'street children' in developing countries are children and young people who are forced on to the street for economic reasons. The majority of these children and young people still live with their family but spend time on the streets in order to earn money (Council of Europe, 1993). A smaller proportion are young people who have become detached from their families and communities and literally live on the streets. There may well be similarities between this latter group and those young people in the UK who experience lengthy periods of detachment (see Chapter 2). There is therefore some potential for cross-over learning from work with young people on the streets in economically poorer countries, and an example of this is provided later in this appendix. However, given the very different nature of the phenomenon in economically affluent countries, the material that follows concentrates primarily on various models of working with young people that have been developed in these countries.

Much of the material presented here relates to the USA which, in many ways, has been at the forefront of the development of services for young people who run away or are on the streets. Some isolated projects began to work with this target group in the late 1960s and early 1970s. However, the key landmark in developments in the USA was the passage of the Runaway and Homeless Youth Act in 1974. This Act was the result of recognition that young people ran away due to problems at home, rather than for adventure, and that there was a lack of a safety net to engage with these young people and work with them on the problems they were facing. The Runaway and Homeless Youth Act led to the set up of a federally-funded network of projects to work with young runaways throughout the USA.

The material that follows is organised into two sections: the first looks at alternative models of working with young people and the second looks at broader trends and issues in the development of work with young runaways.

Alternative models

Schools-based preventive initiatives

Given the fact that running away generally stems from other problems in young people's lives, many initiatives targeted at issues within the family, school and personal spheres can play a preventive role with regard to running away. However, some specific initiatives have been developed in North America which aim directly to prevent the incidence of running away.

In the USA, the National Runaway Switchboard has developed a curriculum that schools staff can use with young people. The purpose of the curriculum is:

> '... to help young people acquire skills that will help them communicate more effectively, learn to seek out trusted adult resources for help, find ways to manage daily stress, and understand what it's like to live on the street. The program is designed to have youth interact with adult service professionals so that in times of crisis, they will feel more comfortable seeking outside help.'

There is also a component aimed at raising awareness among parents.

The curriculum and associated materials are freely available from the National Runaway Switchboard website (www.nrscrisisline.org).

In Canada, a number of peer-helper initiatives have been developed which are aimed at preventing running away. These have tended to involve young people who have experience of running away or being on the streets in informing or assisting young people in schools who may be at risk of being in this situation. Many of these schemes are listed in Caputo, Weiler and Green (1996), which also contains a summary of guidelines for the running of peer-helper initiatives. It is possible to access this document at the Health Canada website (www.hc-sc.gc.ca).

Alternative ways of engaging with young people

Most of the ways employed by projects in other countries to make contact with young people who run away are broadly similar to those already employed in the UK, including telephone contacts, street work and other forms of outreach, and drop-in centres.

An alternative approach developed in the USA is Project Safe Place. This scheme, which was started by the YMCA in Kentucky in 1983, has since been replicated throughout the USA. It involves setting up Safe Place sites, displaying a logo in shops, community facilities, and so on. These are places where young people can go for immediate help if they are in a crisis situation. Staff at participating establishments receive training in dealing with young people and have contacts with resources, such as local runaway shelters, that can offer them immediate help.

Further information about this scheme can be found at www.iglou.com/safeplace.

Provision of accommodation

There are many shelters and refuges in the USA providing temporary accommodation for young people along similar lines to the refuges developed in the UK. It seems common for these projects to work to a 14-day timescale, as in the UK.

An alternative model of emergency accommodation is the 'host home' model run by The Bridge over Troubled Waters in Boston. This model uses volunteer families to provide short-term accommodation for young people, along similar lines to the Night Stop schemes working with over-16-year-olds in the UK. Information about this scheme is contained in an article to be found at www.ncfy.com/bridgfin.htm.

Given the discussion in Chapters 3 and 6 regarding the provision, with parental consent, of temporary accommodation for young people, it is interesting to note the existence of a community boarding programme in Bayside, Australia which provides this service together with family reconciliation work. (Crane and Braddock, 1996)

Street work

Many street-work services in North America appear to offer a more extensive range of services than those developed in the UK. There appears often to be a strong emphasis on the provision of health and practical assistance to young people on the streets. Projects employ means such as mobile vans in conjunction with health professionals.

Integrated models

One of the key features of many projects in North America which distinguish them from the UK projects is their comprehensive nature. A number of examples have been identified of projects that offer a wide range of inter-linked services with the aim of providing a comprehensive solution to the multiple problems faced by many young runaways.

Bridge Emergency Youth Services in Texas (see www.ncfy.com.texas2.htm) offers emergency youth shelter, host homes, family preservation services, street outreach, specific work aimed at young people from minority ethnic backgrounds and a tranisitional living programme for 16- and 17-year-olds.

Girls and Boys Town of Central Florida provides emergency shelter, fostering, long-term residential work, a parenting programme, children in need and family in need services, and runs a Safe Place scheme (see www.ffbh.boystown.org/aboutus/locations/cflorida.htm).

Youth Care in Seattle (www.youthcare.org) offers emergency shelter, longer-term residential, care and educational programmes, counselling and health services, a teen-parent programme, and a transitional living programme.

Broader issues

There are some notable trends in the work being carried out with young runaways in North America which are relevant in terms of considering future development of work with this target group in the UK.

Longer-term work

A number of examples of projects have been identified (including those listed above) which undertake much longer-term work with young people than is common in the UK. Emergency shelter services are often linked with individual counselling and therapeutic programmes which aim to resolve the underlying problems being faced by young people. There also seems to be a strong emphasis in the USA on transitional living programmes, stemming from a recognition of the links between running away and homelessness. These projects assist young people over 16 to move into independent living.

An emphasis on longer-term work is also evident in projects in Denmark and the Netherlands that are described in a review of European street children (Council of Europe, 1996).

Youth development perspective

An important aspect of the US runaway initiatives is their adoption of a 'youth development' perspective to their work. This perspective is outlined in a report by the Family and Youth Services Bureau, which can be obtained from www.ncfy.com/compend.htm. The emphasis of this approach is on facilitating young people to develop skills and competence. The four core components, set out in the above report, are:

- Viewing young people and families as partners rather than as clients, and involving them in designing and delivering programs and services
- Giving all youths access both to prevention and intervention services and to programs that meet their developmental needs
- Directing programs and services to all young people, rather than targeting only those in at-risk situations
- Offering youth opportunities to develop relationships with caring, supportive adults.

There are interesting parallels here with developments within UK projects working with runaways, and the social care sector in general, towards involving young people more in all aspects of service development and provision.

An emphasis on cultural competence

As the range of interventions in the USA has developed, there has been an increased recognition of the potential for projects to fail to meet the needs of the culturally-diverse group of young people who run away or live on the streets, and this has led to initiatives to enhance the cultural competence of projects and staff working with this target group. The cultural competence approach is concerned with meeting the needs of people from all backgrounds and emphasises the need for this to be seen as a dynamic, ongoing process rather than as a goal or outcome.

The Family and Youth Services Bureau has published a guide to enhancing cultural competence of runaway and homeless youth programmes, which is available at www.acf.dhhs.gov/programs/fysb. It sets out a recommended process for enhancing cultural competence and includes a set of questionnaires to assess current cultural competence and an extensive list of source materials.

Links with education

Links with education are a feature of many of the projects identified in other countries. These links are evidenced in a number of ways, such as the tendency to focus preventive efforts in schools settings and the inclusion of education as a programme element in some schemes (e.g., Youth Care in Seattle), both of which were discussed earlier in this appendix.

Another manifestation of these links is the adoption of empowerment-oriented educational models more commonly associated with work with street children in developing countries. An example of this latter approach is the Rising Youth for Social Equity project which was initiated in San Francisco in 1996, based on the Brazilian model of popular education (see www.icrichild.org/projects/ryse.html and www.cydjournal.org/NewDesigns).

The aim of the project is to create 'a well-structured educational, democratic and safe space for street youth to develop language to communicate their experiences and tools to transform their own realities.'

Collaboration

Finally, there is a notable emphasis on collaborative inter-agency approaches to tackling the problems faced by young people who run away in the USA. A number of examples have been found of local and regional initiatives which aim to develop co-operative relationships between runaway services and statutory services. For example, the Massachusetts Youth Development State Collaboration Project (described in www.acf.dhhs.gov/programs/fysb/State-YD-Collb.htm) aims to 'increase collaboration among Massachusetts youth-serving systems and facilitate communication between State and community agencies and systems of care'. An initiative to build co-operation between law-enforcement agencies and runaway and homeless youth centres in Arizona is described in Chapter 6 of a 'Compendium of Critical Issues and Innovative Approaches in Youth Services' accessible at www.ncfy.com/compend.htm.

BIBLIOGRAPHY

Abrahams C and Mungall R (1992) *Runaways: Exploding the Myths.* London: NCH.

Adlaf E and Zdanowicz Y (1999) 'A Cluster-analytic Study of Substance Problems and Mental Health Among Street Youths', *American Journal of Drug and Alcohol Abuse,* Vol: 25 (4).

Barter C (1996) *Nowhere to Hide: Giving Young Runaways a Voice.* London: Centrepoint/NSPCC.

Booth R, Zhang Y and Kwiatkowski C (1999) 'The challenge of changing drug and sex risk behaviors of runaway and homeless adolescents', *Child Abuse and Neglect,* Vol: 23 (12).

Busen N and Beech B (1997) 'A collaborative model for community-based health care screening of homeless adolescents', *Journal of Professional Nursing,* Vol: 13 (5).

Caputo T, Weiler R & Green L (1996) *Peer Helper Initiatives for out-of-the Mainstream Youth: A Report and Compendium.* Ontario: Health Canada.

Council of Europe (1994) *Les Enfants de la Rue.* Strasbourg: Conseil d'Europe.

Crane P and Brannock J (1996) *Homelessness among Young People in Australia: Early Intervention and Prevention.* Hobart: National Clearinghouse for Youth Studies.

Dangelo L, Brown R, English A, Hein K and Remafedi G (1994) 'HIV-Infection and AIDS in Adolescents – a Position Paper of the Society for Adolescent Medicine' *Journal of Adolescent Health,* Vol: 15 (5).

Ensign J and Santelli J (1998) 'Health status and service use - Comparison of adolescents at a school-based health clinic with homeless adolescents', *Archives of Pediatrics and Adolescent Medicine,* Vol: 152 (1).

Greene J and Ringwalt C (1998) 'Pregnancy among three national samples of runaway and homeless youth', *Journal of Adolescent Health,* Vol: 23 (6).

Greene J, Ennett S and Ringwalt C (1999) 'Prevalence and correlates of survival sex among runaway and homeless youth', *American Journal of Public Health,* Vol: 89 (9).

Molnar B, Shade S, Kral A, Booth R and Watters J (1998) 'Suicidal behavior and sexual/physical abuse among street youth', *Child Abuse and Neglect,* Vol: 22 (3).

Newman C (1989) *Young Runaways.* London: The Children's Society.

Pennbridge J, Mackenzie R and Swofford A (1991) 'Risk Profile of Homeless Pregnant Adolescents and Youth', *Journal of Adolescent Health,* Vol: 12 (7) , 534-538.

Rees G (1993) *Hidden Truths – Young People's Experiences of Running Away.* London: The Children's Society.

Safe on the Streets Research Team (1999) *Still Running – Children on the Streets in the UK*. London: The Children's Society.

Stein M, Rees G and Frost N (1994) *Running – The Risk: Young people on the Streets of Britain Today*. London: The Children's Society.

Unger J, Kipke M, Simon T, Montgomery S and Johnson C (1997) 'Homeless youths and young adults in Los Angeles: Prevalence of mental health problems and the relationship between mental health and substance abuse disorders', *American Journal of Community Psychology*, Vol: 25 (3).

Wade J and Biehal N with Clayden J and Stein M (1998) *Going Missing: Young People Absent from Care*. Chichester: John Wiley and Sons.

The Children's Society

A positive force for change

The Children's Society is one of Britain's leading charities for children and young people. Founded in 1881 as a Christian organisation, The Children's Society reaches out unconditionally to children and young people regardless of race, culture or creed.

Over 100 projects throughout England and Wales

We work with over 40,000 children of all ages, focusing on those whose circumstances have made them particularly vulnerable. We aim to help to stop the spiral into isolation, anger and lost hope faced by so many young people.

We constantly look for effective, new ways of making a real difference

We measure local impact and demonstrate through successful practice that major issues can be tackled and better resolved. The Children's Society has an established track record of taking effective action: both in changing public perceptions about difficult issues such as child prostitution, and in influencing national policy and practice to give young people a better chance at life.

The Children's Society is committed to overcoming injustice wherever we find it

We are currently working towards national solutions to social isolation, lack of education and the long-term problems they cause, through focused work in several areas:

- helping parents whose babies and toddlers have inexplicably stopped eating, endangering their development;
- involving children in the regeneration of poorer communities;
- preventing exclusions from primary and secondary schools;
- providing a safety net for young people who run away from home and care;
- seeking viable alternatives to the damaging effects of prison for young offenders.

The Children's Society will continue to raise public awareness of difficult issues to promote a fairer society for the most vulnerable children in England and Wales. For further information about the work of The Children's Society or to obtain a publications catalogue, please contact:

The Children's Society, Publishing Department,
Edward Rudolf House, Margery Street,
London WC1X 0JL.
Tel. 0207 841 4400. Fax 0207 841 4500.
Website: www.childrenssociety.org.uk

The Children's Society is a registered charity: Charity Registration No. 221124.